The George Washington Biography Lesson

Developed by

George Washington's
MOUNT VERNON
ESTATE & GARDENS

In cooperation with
The Society of the Cincinnati

Dedicated to

Mr. Robert Budd Gibby

whose continued support of and belief in education
has made this program possible.

Table of Contents

FOREWORD

George Washington's name is instantly recognizable; his face is still the most familiar of all figures in American history. But, as we enter the 21st century, Americans seem to know less and less about the remarkable career of the man who was the leader among leaders during the founding of our nation.

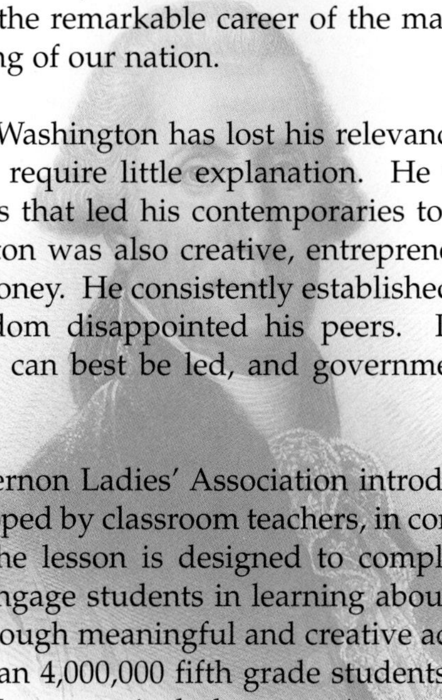

Some may argue that Washington has lost his relevancy; however, many of his best qualities are timeless and require little explanation. He was honest, courageous, and deeply patriotic – qualities that led his contemporaries to call him " The Father of His Country." But, Washington was also creative, entrepreneurial, and generous with his heart, his mind, and his money. He consistently established the highest standards for his own actions, and he seldom disappointed his peers. In short, George Washington demonstrated that armies can best be led, and governments can best be managed by individuals of character.

In 1989, The Mount Vernon Ladies' Association introduced ***The George Washington Biography Lesson***. Developed by classroom teachers, in consultation with Mount Vernon scholars and educators, the lesson is designed to complement the American History curriculum and actively engage students in learning about George Washington and the founding of our nation through meaningful and creative activities. Since then the lesson has been used by more than 4,000,000 fifth grade students in 30 states. In 2000, Mount Vernon has enhanced the Lesson to include new primary document lessons, a lesson on studying George Washington through art, an expanded chapter on George Washington and slavery, and much more. As we enter the 21st century, we believe it is essential that today's students understand the character, strength, and contributions of the first President of the United States and how his legacy remains relevant in our modern world.

Ellen Walton
Regent
The Mount Vernon Ladies' Association

LESSON PLAN: GEORGE WASHINGTON BIOGRAPHY

Purpose of Lesson

To give students accurate biographical information about George Washington and to help them understand how Washington developed the values, principles, and skills that made him an effective leader.

Subsidiary Goals

To highlight events critical to the founding of the United States and its democratic form of government.
To help students understand an individual's responsibilities in our society.
To help students understand the similarities and differences between life in the 18th century and life today.

Prior to starting the lesson, make a list on the chalkboard or poster board of all the things the students know about George Washington. As you complete phases of the lesson, ask your students if any characteristics can be added. Circle all the characteristics the students think make him a good leader. Review the list and make a new list including only the characteristics the students think all good leaders should possess. Have the students use the list to create a definition of a good leader. As you continue to study national or local leaders, evaluate them using this definition.

Strategies for Teaching "A Brief Biography of George Washington" (pp. 10-13)

Review the biography of George Washington (pp.1-9) which has been included to provide you, the teacher, with background information on George Washington's life and career. For additional information on George Washington's changing attitudes toward slavery and life on his Mount Vernon plantation, you should also review the chapter on George Washington and Slavery (pp. 19-27).

Divide the class into four groups, each with comparable reading skills. Assign each group a different page of the Student Biography, giving to each group a copy of the page assigned [the Student Biography pages, (pp. 55-58) are perforated and can be removed easily from the book. They can be laminated for long-term use and returned to the pockets provided in the Teacher Manual]. Ask your students to read and discuss their page as a group, helping each other with the reading if needed. Suggested discussion topics are provided at the bottom of each page of the Student Biography in the Teacher Manual. Have the students find the definitions of the words printed in ***boldface***. After each group has studied their page, ask them to prepare a short summary for the rest of the class. Have the group (or its leader) that read Part I present its summary first, then the group that read Part II, continuing in order to make a chronologically complete biography of George Washington. Also ask each group to talk about the topics they discussed. Each group should be able to assign one or more characteristics from the character list developed by the class prior to the lesson, which they feel describe George Washington. Primary documents have been included that you can use to supplement this portion of the George Washington Biography Lesson.

After the students have finished analyzing the biography of George Washington, distribute the scratch and learn cards. The correct answer to each statement can be found in the Student Biography. Have the students complete the cards in the way you think will be most effective: working individually, in groups, with the Biography, or without. If all answers are completed correctly, the card will spell WASHINGTON.

The Teacher Manual contains a number of subsidiary lesson materials that you can use to outline additional classroom discussion with your students. Each section includes discussion questions that will help with group work and assist your students in analyzing George Washington's character and contributions to the founding of the nation. For ease in reading and comprehension, several sections are printed in a two-column format.

At the completion of the lesson, distribute one trading card to each student in the class. Each card contains "stats" on George Washington either as a farmer, leader, family man, commander in chief, or president.

Classroom Activities

1. Review the list of leadership characteristics your class developed and have the students discuss how the characteristics are important for them personally in making decisions and interacting with others at home and in school.
2. At the conclusion of the lesson, have your students prepare a dictionary of each word they found in ***boldface***. Ask each student to write a paragraph about a topic they have studied in the lesson using three of the words they have researched.

GEORGE WASHINGTON - A BIOGRAPHY FOR TEACHERS

GEORGE WASHINGTON'S CHILDHOOD

1732-1746

Site of Washington's Birthplace

George Washington was born at his father's plantation on Popes Creek in Westmoreland County, Virginia, on February 22, 1732. His father, Augustine Washington, was a leading planter in the area and also served as a justice of the county court. His first wife, Jane Butler, who died in 1729, left Augustine with two sons, Lawrence and Augustine, Jr. , and a daughter, Jane. The elder Augustine married George's mother, Mary Ball, in 1731. George was the eldest of their six children.

In 1735 Augustine moved the family up the Potomac River to another Washington home, Little Hunting Creek Plantation (later renamed Mount Vernon). In 1738 they moved again to Ferry Farm, a plantation on the Rappahannock River near Fredericksburg, Virginia where George spent much of his youth. Little is known of Washington's childhood and it remains the most poorly understood part of his life. Popular fables illustrating his youthful honesty, piety, and physical strength have long taken the place of documented fact. Some of these fables are more plausible than others. The story that Washington threw a silver dollar across the Potomac River—an impossible feat—had its origins in the recollections of a cousin that George could throw a stone across the much narrower Rappahannock River. But others, including the familiar story of Washington and the cherry tree, seem to have been invented by one of Washington's first biographers, Mason Locke Weems.

When George was eleven years old, Augustine died, leaving most of his property to George's older half-brothers. The income from what remained was just sufficient to maintain Mary Washington and her children. As the oldest child, George undoubtedly helped his mother manage the Rappahannock River plantation where they lived. There he learned the importance of hard work and efficiency—practical lessons he carried with him through life.

Lawrence Washington

Little is known about George's formal education. Commonly, the children of Virginia gentry were taught at home by private tutors, or in local private schools. Boys generally began their formal education around the age of seven with lessons focusing on reading, writing, and basic arithmetic. Later they were taught Latin and Greek, as well as practical subjects such as geometry, bookkeeping, and surveying. Wealthy planters often sent their sons to England to finish their schooling, as was done with George's two elder brothers, Lawrence and Augustine. The death of their father, however, made that an impossibility for George Washington. He may have attended a school near his home for the first few years. Later he went to another school, either in Fredericksburg, Stafford County, or Westmoreland County. He excelled in mathematics and learned the rudiments of surveying. But he was not taught Latin or Greek, like many gentleman's sons, and he never learned any foreign language. Nor did he attend college. His formal education ended around the age of 15. Among the gentry class, strong social skills were also considered an essential part of a young man's or woman's education. After the death of their father, George began to spend a great deal of time with his older half-brother, Lawrence, at his home, Mount Vernon. Lawrence became a mentor to his younger brother, tutoring him in his studies, teaching him social graces, and helping to introduce him into society.

Throughout his life, Washington regarded his education as "defective." He consciously made up for some of what he did not learn in school through reading and study on his own. Over the years, he amassed a large and diverse library and in his later years he subscribed to several newspapers. He became a skilled and prolific writer. Perhaps as a result of his lack of formal education, he strongly believed in the value of a good education throughout his life, and left money in his will for the establishment of a school in Alexandria, Virginia, as well as money for a national university.

Young Man Washington

1746-1759

In 1746 Lawrence proposed that George Washington join the British navy. Although George was excited at the idea of a military career, Mary Washington refused her consent, and George was spared the harsh discipline of a life at sea. Despite missing the opportunity of traveling the world, George Washington's young adulthood nevertheless became one of the great adventure stories of American history.

Washington: The Surveyor's Assistant

Young Washington applied himself to surveying, a valuable skill in a colony where land was being settled constantly. In 1748 he joined a surveying expedition to western Virginia at the invitation of Lawrence's neighbors, the powerful Fairfax family. The next year the Fairfaxes helped secure him an appointment as a county surveyor. By the age of 17 he was well on his way to a successful and profitable career. In an effort to establish himself as a landowner and a member of the gentry class, he worked hard, saved his money, and bought unclaimed land.

In 1751 he accompanied Lawrence, who was suffering from tuberculosis, on a voyage to the British island colony of Barbados. Lawrence hoped the tropical air would ease his suffering. While in Barbados Washington saw some of the most extensive fortifications in British America and socialized with military men, experiences that probably stimulated his interest in military service. He also contracted smallpox. Though he recovered quickly, the illness may have rendered him unable to have children.

Lawrence died in 1752, and shortly thereafter George inherited Mount Vernon. He also obtained Lawrence's place in the Virginia militia, and received a major's commission—the first step in his military career.

In 1753 the governor of Virginia, Robert Dinwiddie, learned that French troops had moved south from Canada and were constructing forts in the region south of Lake Erie, an area claimed by Virginia (now in western Pennsylvania). Both France and England recognized the commercial potential of the region. French trappers had been working in the area for some time and Dinwiddie was concerned that the French troops would also fortify the forks of the Ohio—the strategic point where the Allegheny and Monongahela rivers join to form the Ohio River. This point (now Pittsburgh) was the eastern gateway to the Ohio Valley.

Washington Crossing the Allegheny

In the fall of 1753 Dinwiddie sent twenty-one year old Major Washington to deliver a message to the French, demanding they leave the area. With the help of a frontier guide and local Indians, Washington reached the French fort, Duquesne, with Dinwiddie's message. The return trip tested Washington's endurance. He hiked for days through snowy woods, fell off a raft into the ice-choked Allegheny River, nearly drowned, and was forced to spend a freezing night on an island without shelter. His guide, an experienced backwoodsman, suffered frostbite. Washington suffered no ill effects. Washington's account of the arduous 900 mile journey was published by Governor Dinwiddie in both Williamsburg and

London, establishing an international reputation for George Washington by the time he was 22.

A few months later Dinwiddie dispatched Washington, now a lieutenant colonel, and some 150 men to assert Virginia's claims. As they advanced, Washington's men skirmished with French soldiers, killing ten men, including the French commander. Washington then retreated to an ill-placed and poorly constructed makeshift palisade he called Fort Necessity, but was forced to surrender when the French surrounded the fort. The campaign ended in humiliation for Washington, and ignited the French and Indian War.

Washington resigned his commission after the surrender, but returned to the frontier in 1755 as a volunteer aide to General Edward Braddock, the British general sent to lead an expedition to drive the French from the Ohio Country. Braddock's army was routed near the Monongahela River and fled in confusion to Virginia. During the battle Washington had two horses shot from under him and four bullet holes shot through his coat attempting to rally the British soldiers. Although he behaved with conspicuous bravery, Washington could do little except lead the broken survivors to safety.

Colonel George Washington of the Virginia Militia

In recognition of his conduct, Washington was given command of Virginia's entire military force. With a few hundred men he was ordered to protect a frontier some 350 miles long. It was a frustrating assignment but provided him with experience in commanding troops through an arduous campaign. In 1758 the British finally took the forks of the Ohio. Peace returned to Virginia, and Washington resigned his commission to return to Mount Vernon, his duty faithfully performed.

Although barely twenty-seven years old, he was the most experienced native military officer in Virginia. In 1759 he married Martha Dandridge Custis, the young widow of one of the wealthiest men in the colony. He retired to his plantation with many of his early ambitions satisfied. He could hardly have imagined that his greatest adventures lay ahead.

Gentleman Farmer

1759-1775

George Washington spent the years between 1759 and 1775 as a gentleman farmer at Mount Vernon. He worked constantly to improve and expand the mansion house and the plantation that surrounded it. He established himself as an innovative farmer who switched from tobacco to wheat as his main cash crop in the 1760s. In an effort to improve his farming operation, he diligently experimented with new crops, fertilizers, crop rotation, tools, and the breeding of livestock. He also expanded the work of the plantation to include flour milling and commercial fishing in an effort to make Mount Vernon a more profitable estate. By the time of his death in 1799, he had expanded the plantation from 2,000 to 8,000 acres consisting of five farms, with more than 3,000 acres under cultivation.

Building Mount Vernon

Although most of this time was dedicated to his private affairs and family life with his wife Martha and her two children, Washington continued to participate in public life. He was elected to the House of Burgesses in 1758 (after being defeated twice) and served several terms. He viewed the growing disputes between Britain and the American colonies with deep concern. He was not a political firebrand, stirring orator, or cloakroom deal-maker, but he impressed his peers as a modest, dependable man of strength and good sense.

In the fall of 1774, Washington was chosen as one of seven Virginia representatives to the Continental Congress. Upon his arrival in Philadelphia other delegates immediately recognized him as a man of patriotic views and sound judgment. At six feet three inches tall, he towered over the other delegates, and he had an athletic grace and commanding presence that impressed everyone he met. Although Washington spoke very little in Congress, many of the delegates noticed what one called his " easy, soldier-like air."

Commander-in-Chief

1775-1783

In June 1775, Congress commissioned George Washington to take command of the Continental Army besieging the British in Boston. He wrote home to Martha that he expected to "return safe to you in the fall." The command kept him away from Mount Vernon for more than eight years.

It was a command for which his military background, though greater than that of any of the other available candidates, hardly prepared him. His knowledge lay in frontier warfare, involving relatively small numbers of soldiers. He had no practical experience maneuvering large formations, handling cavalry or artillery, or maintaining supply lines adequate to support thousands of men in the field. He learned on the job, and although his army reeled from one misfortune to another, he had the courage, determination, and mental agility to keep the American cause one step ahead of complete disintegration until he figured out how to win the unprecedented revolutionary struggle he was leading.

Washington Taking Command of the American Army

His task was not overwhelming at first. The British position in Boston was untenable, and in March 1776 they withdrew from the city. But it was only a temporary respite. In June a new British army, under the command of Sir William Howe, arrived in the colonies with orders to take New York City. Howe commanded the largest expeditionary force Britain had ever sent overseas.

Defending New York was almost impossible. An island city, New York is surrounded by a maze of waterways that gave a substantial advantage to an attacker with naval superiority. Howe's army was larger, better equipped, and far better trained than Washington's. They defeated Washington's army at Long Island in August, and routed the Americans a few weeks later at Kip's Bay, resulting in the loss of the city. Compelled to retreat northward, Washington was defeated again at White Plains. The American defense of New York City came to a humiliating conclusion on November 16, 1776, with the surrender of Fort Washington and some 2,800 men. Washington ordered his army to retreat across New Jersey. The remains of his forces, mud-soaked and exhausted, crossed the Delaware River into Pennsylvania on December 7.

The British had good reason to believe that the American rebellion would be over in a few months, and that Congress, which had fled to Baltimore, would seek peace rather than face complete subjugation of the colonies. The enlistments of most of Washington's army were due to expire at the end of December.

However, instead of crushing the remains of Washington's army, Howe went into winter quarters, with advanced garrisons at Trenton and Princeton, leaving Washington open to execute one of the most daring military operations in American history. On Christmas night Washington's troops crossed the Delaware and attacked the unsuspecting garrison at Trenton, forcing it to surrender. A few days later Washington again crossed the Delaware, outmaneuvered the force sent to crush him, and fell on the enemy at Princeton, inflicting a humiliating loss on surprised British regulars.

Though the victories were not militarily decisive, this proved to be the pivotal moment of the war. Washington had inflicted little damage on the British army. Howe still enjoyed a numerical superiority, and there was nothing about these modest victories to suggest that the Americans were capable of defeating the British army in a pitched battle. Trenton and Princeton instead marked a watershed in the way George Washington conceptualized the war. He began to see the war as a political problem as much as a military one. The enthusiastic response to the victories at Trenton and Princeton taught him the importance of public opinion to sustaining a popular war of resistance. Washington had little conventional military education to discard. In an unconventional conflict, he learned from experiences that perplexed and frustrated his opponents. The truth of the situation—that the American rebellion would not end until Washington's army was destroyed—ran against the established conventions of European warfare. Howe never seems to have abandoned the belief that once the Americans were deprived of their major cities, the rebellion would wither. In the summer of 1777, he mounted an offensive against Philadelphia. Washington moved to defend the city, and was defeated at the Battle of Brandywine. Philadelphia fell two weeks later. An American counterattack on the main British camp at Germantown, just outside the city, was repulsed, but not without demonstrating that Washington and his army, if outmaneuvered and outfought, still possessed considerable fighting spirit.

Washington Crossing the Delaware

Gradually it occurred to the British high command that capturing Philadelphia meant very little. The supplies that had flowed to Washington's men through the city simply flowed to them through other channels. Rather than ceasing operations, Congress simply packed up and moved to another town. Philadelphia was no more essential to the American cause than New York City. Howe was relieved of command early in 1778, and his replacement, Sir Henry Clinton, was ordered to evacuate Philadelphia.

Clinton decided to return to New York by land, in a rapid retreat through the unsparing heat of the Middle Atlantic summer. Washington planned a quick blow at Clinton's flank and attacked the British near Monmouth Court House, New Jersey. The Battle of Monmouth, although a tactical standoff, proved that the Continental Army could stand up to British regulars in the open field without the element of surprise. It also confirmed Washington's position as the pre-eminent American military leader, and energized the patriot cause.

British Surrender at Yorktown

For much of the remainder of the war, Washington's most important strategic task was to keep the British bottled up in New York. He never gave up hope of retaking the city, but he was not willing to risk the army without a fair prospect of success. An alliance with France and the arrival of a French army under the Comte de Rochambeau in July 1780 renewed Washington's hopes for a successful operation to recapture New York; however, Washington and Rochambeau commanded about 9,000 men—some 5,000 fewer than Clinton. Together the allied generals concluded that an attack on New York could not succeed.

They decided, instead, to strike at the British army under Cornwallis, which was camped at Yorktown, Virginia. Washington's planning was as bold as before Trenton and Princeton, but on a much larger scale. Depending on Clinton's inactivity, Washington marched south to lay siege to Cornwallis. On October 19, 1781, he accepted the surrender of Cornwallis' army. Although two more years passed before a treaty of peace was completed, the victory at Yorktown effectively brought the Revolutionary War to an end.

To the amazement of the world, Washington had prevailed over the more numerous, better-supplied and fully trained British army because he was more flexible than his opponents. He learned that it was more important to keep his army intact and win an occasional victory to rally public opinion than it was to hold American cities or defeat the British army in the open field. Revolutionary leaders in every part of the world have successfully employed this insight over the last two hundred years, but never with a result as startling as Washington's victory over the British.

AMERICAN CINCINNATUS

1783-1789

Having secured victory in the field, Washington presented himself before Congress in Annapolis, Maryland, on December 23, 1783, and resigned his commission. Like the hero of Classical antiquity whose conduct he most admired—Cincinnatus, who left his plow to lead the Roman republic to victory and then returned home without accepting rewards for his service—Washington left Annapolis and went home to Mount Vernon, with the fixed intention of never serving in public life again. This one act, without precedent in modern history, made him an international hero.

George Washington as a Farmer

Washington devoted most of his time in the years after the Revolutionary War to rebuilding Mount Vernon, which he had neglected during the war. He experimented with new crops and fertilizers and bred some of the finest mules in the nation. He also served as president of the Potomac Company, which worked to improve the navigation of the river in order to make it easier for upstream farmers to get their produce to market.

Although Washington longed for a peaceful life at Mount Vernon, the affairs of the nation continued to command his attention. He watched with mounting dismay as the weak union created by the Articles of Confederation gradually disintegrated, unable to collect revenue or pay its debts. He was appalled by the excesses of the state legislatures and frustrated by the diplomatic, financial, and military impotence of the Confederation Congress. By 1786 Washington had concluded that reform was essential. What was needed, he wrote to James Madison, was an "energetic Constitution."

Washington Presiding in the Constitutional Convention— 1787

Washington ended his self-imposed retirement in 1787 and traveled to Philadelphia to attend the convention to recommend changes to the Articles of Confederation. He was unanimously chosen to preside over the Constitutional Convention, a job that took four months. He spoke very little in the convention, but few delegates were more determined to devise a government endowed with real energy and authority. " My wish," he wrote, "is that the convention may adopt no temporizing expedients, but probe the defects of the Constitution to the bottom, and provide a radical cure."

After the convention adjourned, Washington's reputation and support were essential to overcome opposition to the ratification of the proposed Constitution. He worked for months to rally support for the new instrument of government. It was a difficult struggle. Even in Washington's native Virginia, the Constitution was ratified by a majority of only one vote.

Once the Constitution was approved, Washington hoped he would be allowed to retire again to private life. But when the first presidential election was held, Washington received a vote from every presidential elector. He remains the only president in American history to be elected by the unanimous voice of the people.

President Washington

1789-1797

Washington served two terms as president. His first term (1789-1793) was occupied primarily with organizing the executive branch of the new government and establishing administrative procedures that made it possible for the government to operate with the energy and efficiency he believed were essential to the future of the republic. An astute judge of talent, he surrounded himself with the most able men in the new nation. Washington appointed his former aide-de-camp, Alexander Hamilton, as Secretary of the Treasury. Thomas Jefferson served as Secretary of State, and his former artillery chief, Henry Knox was the first Secretary of War. James Madison was one of Washington's principle advisors.

The Inauguration of George Washington

In his First Inaugural Address, Washington confessed that he was "unpracticed in the duties of civil administration," but he was one of the most able administrators ever to serve as president. He administered the government with fairness and integrity, assuring Americans that the president could exercise extensive executive authority without corruption, and he executed the laws with restraint, establishing precedents for broad-ranging presidential authority. "His integrity was most pure," Thomas Jefferson wrote, "his justice the most inflexible I have ever known, no motive of interest or consanguinity, friendship or hatred, being able to bias his decision." Washington set a standard for presidential integrity rarely met by his successors, though he established an ideal by which they all are judged.

During Washington's first term, the federal government adopted a series of measures proposed by Alexander Hamilton to resolve the escalating debt crisis and established the nation's finances on a sound basis, concluded peace treaties with the southeastern Indian tribes, and designated a site on the Potomac River for the permanent capital of the United States. But as Washington's first term ended, a bloody Indian war continued on the northwestern frontier. The warring tribes were encouraged by the British, who retained military posts in the northwest in defiance of the treaty of peace. The Spanish denied Americans the use to the Mississippi River. These problems limited the westward expansion to which Washington was committed.

Growing partisanship within the government also concerned Washington. Many men in the new government—including Thomas Jefferson, James Madison, and other leaders of the emerging Republican party—were opposed to Hamilton's financial program. Washington despised political partisanship, but he could do little to slow the development of political parties.

During his first term Washington toured the northern and southern states, and found that the new government enjoyed the general support of the American people. Convinced that the government could get along without him, he planned to step down at the end of his first term. But the members of his cabinet convinced him that he alone could command the respect of members of both burgeoning political parties. Thomas Jefferson visited Washington at Mount Vernon to urge him to accept a second term. Although longing to return home permanently, Washington reluctantly agreed.

Washington's second term (1793-1797) was dominated by foreign affairs and marred by a deepening partisanship in his own administration. Washington assumed the presidency on the eve of the French Revolution, a time of great international crisis. The outbreak of a general European war in 1793 forced the crisis to the center of American politics. Washington believed the national interest of the United States dictated neutrality. War would be disastrous for commerce and shatter the nation's finances. The future of the country depended on the increase in wealth and opportunity that would come with commerce and westward expansion. One of Washington's most important accomplishments was keeping the United States out of the war, giving the new nation an opportunity to grow in strength, while establishing the principle of neutrality that shaped American foreign policy for more than a century.

Although Washington's department heads agreed that the United States should remain neutral, disagreements over foreign policy aggravated partisan tensions among them. The disagreements were part of the deepening division between Federalists and Republicans. Opposition to federal policies developed into resistance to the law in 1794, as distillers in Western Pennsylvania rioted and refused to pay taxes. Washington directed the army to restore order—a step applauded by Federalists and condemned by Republicans.

Partisan tensions reached a height during the last years of Washington's presidency. To secure peace with Britain, Washington sent Chief Justice John Jay to London to negotiate a treaty. The treaty was extremely unpopular with Republicans, who charged that Washington himself had become a tool of Britain. Few things ever troubled Washington more deeply than these attacks on his character.

Despite Washington's disappointment with the rise of partisanship, the last years of his presidency were marked by important achievements. The long Indian war on the northwest frontier was won, Britain surrendered its forts in the northwest, and Spain opened the Mississippi to American commerce. These accomplishments opened the West to settlement.

WASHINGTON IN RETIREMENT

1797-1799

By 1796 Washington was ready for retirement, and no one could persuade him to accept a third term. With the help of Alexander Hamilton, he composed his " Farewell Address" to the American people, which urged his fellow citizens to cherish the Union and avoid partisanship and permanent foreign alliances. In March 1797, he turned the government over to John Adams and returned to Mount Vernon, determined to live his last years as a simple gentleman farmer.

In 1798, events conspired to draw him again into the public arena. President John Adams named Washington commanding general of a provisional army to be raised to defend the republic against a perceived French invasion. For several months Washington devoted himself to organizing the officer corps, but he refused to assume another public role, and rejected a suggestion that he stand for president again in 1800.

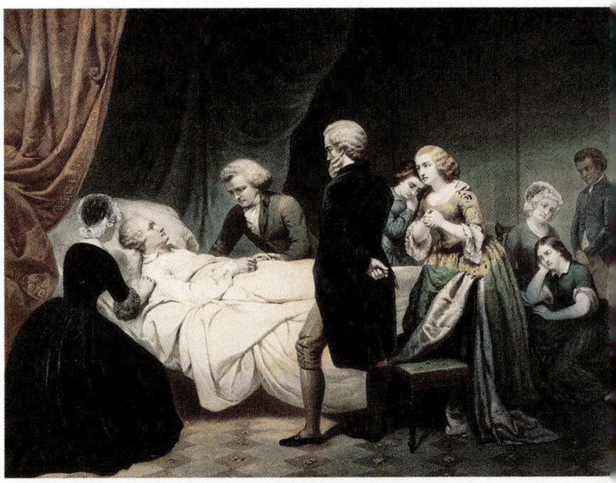

The Death of Washington

On December 12, 1799, he was caught out in sleet and snow while riding over his farms. The resulting illness progressed rapidly and Washington suffered with a throat inflammation that made breathing extremely painful. Doctors arrived early on the morning of December 14, but there was little they could do to ease Washington's pain. He faced death with characteristic courage, saying, " I die hard, but I am not afraid to go." With his wife at his side, George Washington died around 10:00 p.m. on December 14, 1799. Four days later a solemn funeral was held at Mount Vernon.

Mock Funeral, held in Philadelphia, Pennsylvania

As news of his death spread, the nation plunged into mourning. Mock funerals were held in major cities and small towns. Hurried into print were hundreds of eulogies and orations lamenting the loss of the "great and good" Washington. Many feared his loss, however, Washington believed that the new nation had developed the character and strength to survive.

George Washington has been acclaimed for two hundred years as the indispensable man of our Revolution. But he secured immortality by insisting that he was dispensable. He asserted that the cause of liberty was larger than any individual.

"It should be the highest ambition of every American," Washington wrote, "to extend his views beyond himself, and to bear in mind that his conduct will not only affect himself, his country, and his immediate posterity; but that its influence may be co-extensive with the world, and stamp political happiness or misery on ages yet unborn." This call to his fellow citizens was meant for each of us as well.

JACK D. WARREN, JR.

FAST FACTS

When was George Washington born? On the day of his birth, the calendar date was February 11, 1731. However, in September of 1752, the colonies converted from the Gregorian calendar to the Julian calendar. This change required adding eleven days to each year, changing the old date of February 11 to February 22. In addition, the beginning of the new year was moved from March 1 to January 1. From that year on, Washington regarded February 22, 1732 as his birthday.

Did George Washington chop down a cherry tree? Young George did not chop down his father's cherry tree. The story was invented in the 19th century by a man named Mason Weems and was printed in the McGuffey Reader, a popular children's textbook. So many generations of school children have read the story of the cherry tree that it has become a legend even though it is not true.

How many direct descendants of George Washington are there? None. George Washington had no children, and thus there are no direct descendants. However, Washington came from a large family and many of his brothers and sisters had children—so the name Washington is common today.

Did George Washington wear a wig? No. From the time he was a young man until his death he wore his hair in military fashion, tied in the back in a small tail or "queue." Like many of his contemporaries who did not want to wear wigs when they became fashionable, he powdered his hair.

Did George Washington have wooden teeth? He had false teeth, but they were not made of wood. What they were made of makes wood sound good. His dentist, Dr. John Greenwood, used a cow's tooth, one of Washington's teeth, hippopotamus ivory, metal, and springs. They fit poorly and always caused him discomfort. No one knows where the story of the wooden teeth originated.

Did George Washington free his slaves? Yes. George Washington became a slave owner at age eleven, when he inherited ten slaves upon the death of his father. As he grew older, and especially as he fought for liberty in the Revolution, his attitude toward slavery changed. He emancipated his slaves in his will and his estate paid pensions to the older African Americans for decades. Washington is the only founding father to free all of his slaves.

A Brief Biography of George Washington

Part I: A Colonial Boyhood

People from many countries settled in early America. Among them was John Washington. He sailed to Virginia from England in 1657 on a ship called the Sea Horse of London. In a few years, John Washington acquired land, married, and began a family. His most famous ***descendant*** was his great-grandson, George Washington, the first President of the United States.

George Washington was born at ten o'clock in the morning on February 22, 1732, in Westmoreland County, Virginia. His parents were Augustine and Mary Ball Washington. George grew up near Fredericksburg, Virginia. He had a younger sister and three younger brothers. He also had two older half brothers who were sent to England to go to school.

Studying was very important. Spelling and handwriting were practiced by writing in a ***copybook***. Children copied the "Rules of Civility," which told them how to behave. George carefully wrote all 110 rules in his copybook which helped him to develop good handwriting. He worked hard and learned about geography, astronomy, arithmetic and ***surveying***.

When George was 11 years old, his father died. George became very close to his older half brother, Lawrence. George liked to visit Lawrence who was living in a small house built on the Potomac River. Lawrence named the house and its farm, Mount Vernon.

George enjoyed listening to Lawrence talk about the time he served in the military with the British. He also liked to hear Lawrence and his friends talk about the Virginia ***frontier***. One day, George learned that Lawrence's friend, George William Fairfax, was going to the frontier to survey land. George wanted to go. He had learned a little about surveying and had practiced by measuring Lawrence's turnip field. Although he was only 16 years old, Mr. Fairfax allowed him to join the group.

George learned more than surveying on the trip. The men rode on horseback for days exploring the wilderness. They slept in the open, still wearing their clothes and rolled up in blankets. They talked with Indians, ate some of their food, and watched them dance in the bright firelight. George wrote about these ***experiences*** in his journal.

Discussion Topics

1. Do you study the same things that Washington did as a boy? What do you study that Washington did not? Why do you think what children study has changed? Do teachers and parents still have rules for good behavior?

2. What do you think Washington's surveying trip was like? Would it be similar to a trip to the Shenandoah Valley today? How would it be different? How do you think Washington crossed rivers? Would there have been roads and hotels?

Also See

Page 14, "Rules of Civility," which provides a facsimile of Washington's boyhood handwriting from the Rules of Civility, with suggested activities

Part II: Starting a Career and Family

George became a good surveyor. He started his own business when he was 17 years old. Because he was honest and fair, many people hired him to survey their lands.

When George was 19, his older half brother, Lawrence, became very ill. Many doctors tried to cure him, but nothing helped. After Lawrence's death, George lived at Mount Vernon.

George joined the Virginia ***militia***. He was sent to the Ohio River on an important mission by the British governor of Virginia. Soon Major Washington was fighting in the first battles of the French and Indian War. The next year, he served as an ***aide*** to the British General Edward Braddock. In a fearful battle, George Washington escaped injury many times. Four bullets ripped through his coat. Two horses were shot from under him. Later, he was made a colonel and led soldiers who ***defended*** Virginia's frontier in the Shenandoah Valley. Finally, after years of battles and a British victory, the war was over.

About this time, Colonel Washington met a young woman named Martha Custis. Her husband had died, leaving her with two small children, Jacky, three years old, and Patsy, one year old. George Washington and Martha Custis were married on January 6, 1759.

The Washingtons were happy at Mount Vernon. Many friends and relatives visited. There were parties and foxhunts. Colonel Washington had already added on to the house and now bought land to increase the size of his plantation. He grew many food crops. He stopped growing tobacco and made wheat and corn his main ***cash crops***.

Colonel Washington was elected to the House of Burgesses and often went to its meetings in the Virginia capital of Williamsburg. He was quiet and thoughtful during the meetings. One person described him as "straight as an Indian,...more than six feet two inches...about 175 pounds." His hair was reddish brown and his eyes were blue. While in Williamsburg, he and Martha would go to concerts and plays. They liked to dance and went to fancy balls at the Governor's Palace.

Discussion Topics

1. Why do you think being honest and fair helped Washington as a surveyor? Would people buy land if they thought it was surveyed incorrectly? Is being honest and fair important for surveyors today? Is it important in other jobs? Why?

2. Why do you think Washington grew many food crops at Mount Vernon? Could he buy food at a grocery store? How was food cooked then? How do you think people kept food from spoiling?

Also see:

Page 15, "1753: George Washington's Mission to the Ohio," for an account of this trip.

Page 19, "George Washington and Slavery," for a discussion of Washington's changing attitude toward slavery that ultimately led him to free his slaves.

George Washington and other colonists were becoming angry with England. Goods from England were expensive and poorly made. In addition, the colonists had to sell their crops to England for very low prices. Finally, England tried to force the colonists to pay higher taxes.

Colonel Washington went to Philadelphia for the First Continental Congress to discuss these problems. The British were told of the colonists' concerns but did nothing. In 1775, Colonel Washington was elected to the Second Continental Congress. By the time it met, battles had been fought at Lexington and Concord in Massachusetts. The American Revolution had started. A military leader was needed. The Congress named George Washington ***Commander in Chief*** of the Continental Army.

The Revolutionary War was long and difficult. General Washington did not have enough soldiers, guns, food, or equipment. He learned from the French and Indian War to make the most of his supplies and keep his men healthy. His men became good soldiers because Washington demanded hard work and ***discipline***. General Washington decided not to attack the British directly. Instead he would move his troops quickly and then strike by surprise. The British could not capture him. The years of fighting finally ended in Yorktown, Virginia, in 1781, when the British General Cornwallis surrendered.

Although the war was won, it was also a sad time for the Washington family. Martha's son, Jacky, died of Camp Fever at Yorktown. Her daughter, Patsy, had died a few years earlier.

In 1783 a peace treaty with England was signed. Some of General Washington's officers wanted him to ***seize*** power and run the new nation, but he refused. Instead he resigned as Commander in Chief, disbanded the Army, and went home to Mount Vernon to live the rest of his life as a private citizen.

However, this was not to be. The 13 new states did not work well together. Soon each state sent delegates to a Constitutional Convention in Philadelphia to solve the problem. General Washington went and asked to ***preside*** over the convention. After weeks of long ***debates*** and many votes, the ***delegates*** worked out their differences. They wrote a new constitution for the nation with a ***democratic*** government. When the time came to elect a new a leader for the new government, George Washington was the ***unanimous*** choice.

Discussion Topics

1. Why do you think Washington's men wanted to seize power? Would they become rich and powerful? What would have happened to other people and to the country? Why do you think Washington stopped his men? What do you think he wanted for the country?
2. Why do you think the states did not work well together? At that time they all had different money and different laws. How would you buy something in another place if your money was not good there? What would be a better solution?

Also See

Page 16, "Rebellion in the Continental Army!" for a mock-up newspaper account of Washington's confrontation with the officers who wanted to seize power.

Part IV: President and Back Home

In New York City on April 30, 1789, George Washington took the oath of office as President of the United States. An excited crowd gave three rousing cheers. Those early years were very important to our new country. President Washington worked very hard to lay a ***foundation*** so the new government would succeed. He created ***departments*** within the government, each with a different job. He made sure that federal laws were obeyed everywhere. He had the government issue money that was good in all the states. President Washington also helped plan a new capital for the nation that was named "Washington" in his honor. Many of his decisions became ***precedents*** that later presidents would follow.

Washington agreed to serve a second term as president, even though he wanted to go home to Mount Vernon. Some people wanted him to be president even longer, but he would not. After eight years he left the office to the newly elected president, John Adams.

Once again a private citizen, he returned home. At last he was able to take care of his ***beloved*** Mount Vernon plantation. Once more family and friends visited for dinner, conversation, and dancing.

General Washington enjoyed quiet evenings on the piazza overlooking the Potomac River. One of Martha's grandchildren , Nelly, often played music for him and his guests. This peaceful life lasted less than three years.

After riding through a bad winter storm, General Washington caught a cold. His throat became ***infected*** making it difficult to breathe. On December 14, 1799, at the age of 67, George Washington died from this infection called ***quinsy***. As he wished, he was buried at Mount Vernon.

People everywhere ***mourned***. Henry Lee, who had been with Washington in the Revolutionary War, wrote that Washington was"...first in war, first in peace and first in the hearts of his countrymen." General Lee read this ***eulogy*** in Congress. Everyone shared his feelings.

Discussion Topics

1. Why do you think the first years of the new government, when Washington was President, were so important? What would have happened to the country if the government Washington set up had failed? Would that have made a difference to us today? Do you think he was a successful president?

2 Why were people sad when Washington died? How can someone be "first in war" and "first in peace" at the same time? What do these words mean? If you were to write a Eulogy for yourself, what would it be?

Also See

"The Reluctant President," page 17, for a discussion of Washington's feelings about being elected president.

Rules of Civility

George Washington had excellent handwriting. As a boy he practiced copying ***The Rules of Civility and Decent Behavior in Company and Conversation.*** The copy below shows how Washington wrote the first four of these rules. His original was written when he was about 12 years old and is in the Library of Congress in Washington D.C. The rules, which numbered 110, were also a model for good behavior and manners when he was growing up.

Notice that in Washington's time more words were capitalized than are today. You will also see that the spelling of some words have changed and that sometimes a letter which looks like our "f" was used as an "s."

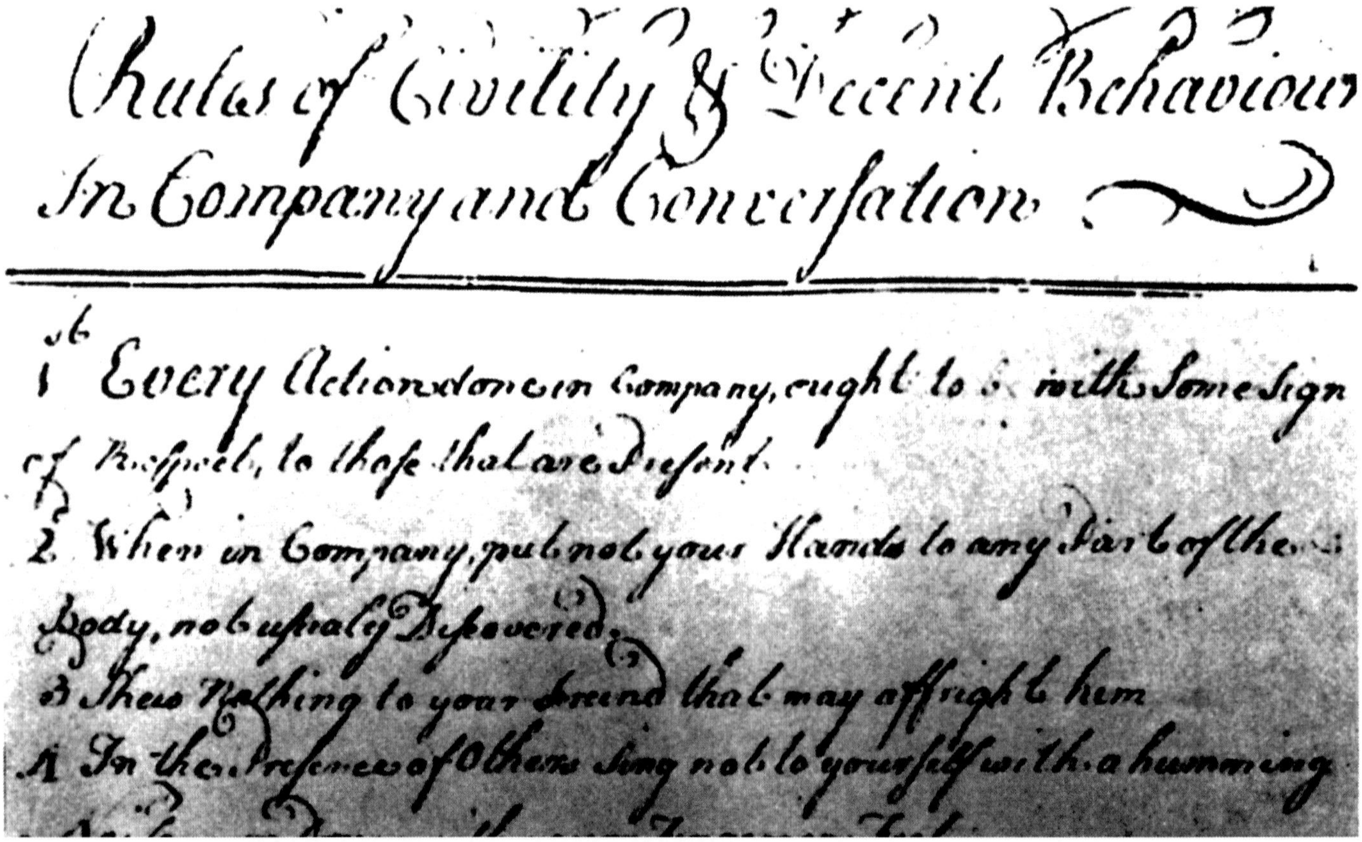

1st Every action done in company, ought to be with Some Sign of Respect, to those that are Present.

2 When in Company, put not your Hands to any Part of the Body, not usually Discovered.

3 Shew Nothing to your Freind that may affright him.

4 In the Presence of Others Sing not to yourself with a humming Noise, nor Drum with your Fingers or Feet.

<u>*Suggested Activities*</u>

1. Have the students copy these rules in their best handwriting. Have the students write the rules with a quill pen, as Washington did. What would they change or add if they were to make "Rules of Civility" for today?
2. Have students work in small groups to develop short skits illustrating the things that Washington's list says you are not to do in company. Discuss why these things might be considered impolite.

1753: George Washington's Mission to the Ohio

England and France were locked in a world-wide cold war in 1753, each trying to gain an advantage over the other. In North America, they both wanted the Ohio River Valley, an area where few Europeans had ventured at the time.

The French reached the Ohio River Valley first, following a route that led from their Canadian colonies, across Lake Erie and then south by river. The English had not yet gotten there, but had claimed some of its lands through the "Ohio Company," a business venture formed by powerful Englishmen, including the highest royal official in Virginia, Governor Robert Dinwiddie.

When Dinwiddie learned that the French were moving into the Ohio River Valley, he sought help from the King. King George II's response was strong: first, he ordered, send an envoy to tell the French to leave, then build a fort in the area and, if necessary, use force to drive the French out.

Choosing the **envoy** to carry the message to the French was a problem: the person had to be able to handle a diplomatic mission, and be able to make his way through hundreds of miles of Indian-occupied wilderness. George Washington, only 21 at the time, rode to Williamsburg and volunteered for the mission, using his contacts with the Fairfax family (who were shareholders in the Ohio Company) and citing his surveying experience in the Blue Ridge Mountains and the Shenandoah Valley. Washington was appointed to the job on October 31, 1753.

He set out the same day, hiring a guide, a French **interpreter** and four others along the way. By the 22nd of November, Washington's group had reached the Forks of the Ohio—where the Monongahela and Allegheny Rivers came together to form the Ohio. With his surveyor's eye, Washington noted that the forks were "...extremely well situated for a Fort, as it has the absolute Command of both Rivers." (The French built Fort Duquesne there the next year, and eventually it became the site of Pittsburgh).

Washington then went to Logtown, an Indian town, to meet with the Iroquois chief, "Half-King." Because of an earlier treaty between the British and the Iroquois, Half-King and several other chiefs joined Washington, traveling to Venango, where he first encountered the French. There he was told to continue to Fort Le Boeuf, on the head waters of French Creek, which was the command of the highest French official in the area, Legardeur de St. Pierre. On the 12th of December, Washington met with St. Pierre, delivering a letter written by Dinwiddie, ordering the French to leave the area. St. Pierre brushed aside the order, and tried to turn the Indians against the British with a promise of guns and supplies.

With St. Pierre's answer in hand, Washington was eager to return to Dinwiddie. The return trip, undertaken in the depths of winter, became a life-or-death adventure. The horses were so weak from hunger that they were abandoned—Washington and one guide set out on foot. Soon they encountered other Indians, **allied** with the French, and one shot at Washington with a rifle.

Now racing through deep snow to stay ahead of Indian pursuers, they reached the Allegheny River in two days. Their attempt to raft the ice-choked river ended in disaster as Washington was knocked overboard in deep water and saved himself only by catching the raft as it swept by. The severe cold that night froze their clothes and the guide's fingers—but also the river, allowing them to walk across on the ice the next morning. Soon they reached the safety of an English trader's settlement.

On January 16, 1754, after completing the return trip to Williamsburg, Washington reported to Governor Dinwiddie. Washington's written report of his remarkable journey, including the information he gathered—that the French were preparing to descend the Allegheny River to the Forks of the Ohio that spring—was published within days in Williamsburg. A London edition soon followed that included a map that was based on Washington's hand-drawn map of the Ohio River Valley. A facsimile of that map is provided (p. 47).

The information set the English in action. Three months later Washington was to lead a force of 160 men back into the area, where he fought what were to be the opening battles of the French and Indian War.

Rebellion in the Continental Army!

March 15, 1783, Newburgh, New York.

An important meeting between George Washington, Commander in Chief of the Continental Army, and his officers occurred today. The men have been extremely unhappy—and have been talking of taking up their guns and bayonets!

The officers are no longer angry at the British. Since the stunning American victory at Yorktown, Virginia, in October of 1781, the British Army has caused little trouble. The remaining forces still occupy New York City, but are quiet. They will not leave until a peace treaty is signed. The peace talks, taking place in Paris, France, are dragging on.

The American soldiers have grown angry with their own country, made up of the thirteen colonies that joined together in the Revolution. With the long wait for peace, the states have fallen far behind in paying the soldiers. Recently, cash has fallen short for such basics as food and clothing, despite the efforts of the Continental Congress.

Some officers have talked about General Washington becoming King of our new nation—he would make things work, they say. But more officers talk of using their weapons to take what is owed to them. Some plan to take over the government and run it themselves!

General Washington called a meeting on March 15, 1783 with these **rebellious** officers. All eyes were on the Commander in Chief as he entered—would he join with them and become King of the United States?

Washington Stands Firm

With his opening words, it was clear that George Washington had no use for **monarchs** and would not become one. Instead he told the men how much he admired them for their sacrifices in winning the Revolution. The General then pointed out that this was now their country. If they used their guns to take what they wanted, he warned, they would be hurting their own families and friends. But the men were too angry to listen.

Washington urged the men not to start a war within the new nation. He asked them to set an example of respect for democracy and law for all. But even this plea fell on deaf ears—the men were too desperate and angry.

Washington Reads Letter

General Washington then told the men of a letter he had just received from a Congressman. The letter promised help. According to Washington, the letter proved that the country would treat them fairly.

General Washington opened the letter to read it aloud. And then something seemed to be wrong with him—he just stared at the letter, as if confused or dazed. In seconds, every man was asking, "What is wrong?" Their anger and desperation seemed unimportant compared with the possibility that Washington, who had led them to victory and inspired them through every defeat, might not be well.

When the room grew quiet, Washington moved again. In a moment of drama and tension, he pulled out a pair of glasses—which no one had seen before. As he put them on, he said, "Gentlemen, you will permit me to put on my spectacles, for I have not only grown gray but almost blind in the service of my country."

Rebels Give Up Their Plans

Those simple words were charged with meaning. The men had never before seen General Washington so humble, and saw clearly his deep **commitment** to our nation and to liberty. They realized how wrong they were in thinking only of themselves. Many wept out of shame. To a man, they gave up their plans to become dictators and promised to obey the laws of our new nation. The meeting ended with our country on the path to democracy!

The Reluctant President

At the end of the Revolution, George Washington voluntarily resigned as Commander in Chief - an act that astounded the world. Most people thought that Washington, the most powerful man in the newly-formed United States, would make himself its ruler. George III, King of England, is said to have exclaimed that Washington was "the greatest man alive."

George Washington resigned because he had promised to do so when he accepted the job in 1775. And he believed firmly in government by law, not by monarchs and dictators. To avoid any suspicions that he might wish to rule as one, Washington not only resigned as Commander in Chief, but announced he would never seek a role in the future government.

Yet his experience in the Revolution convinced him that the new nation needed a strong central government. Otherwise taxes could not be raised for national defense, trade between states would be difficult, and money would not be accepted from one state to another. The **Articles of Confederation,** which the states had agreed upon in 1781 to govern themselves, had little strength. In the years after the Revolution, it was clear that the nation Washington had fought to create was coming apart.

Washington responded by helping those who called for a new Constitution. When the Constitutional Convention was held in 1787, he attended as a **delegate** from Virginia and was quickly elected its presiding officer. His important role helped the Constitution win approval in state after state. Many also wanted Washington to become first president, for who else had proven himself trustworthy with such power?

On February 4, 1789 electors met in each state, cast their votes for president, and sent the sealed ballots to the newly-formed Congress. Although the votes would not be opened and counted for several months, it was widely believed that George Washington would receive the most votes for president.

Yet Washington was reluctant. He did not want to break his earlier promise. In addition, it might look as if he had worked for the new Constitution just to gain power. He also knew the challenges and demands of creating a new government and worried that he may not fully succeed.

His friends pointed out that his promise had been that he would not "seek" office, and he had not campaigned or otherwise worked to get the job of president. Besides, they argued, this new government needed his authority if it were to have any chance of succeeding. It would be far worse for him to refuse to help his country than to worry about misguided criticism about his earlier promise.

The first Congress convened in New York City on March 4, 1789. After a month's delay awaiting a quorum, the sealed ballots were opened and officially counted on April 6, 1789. George Washington was the first choice for President of every elector in every state. He is the only person to be unanimously elected president.

On April 14, 1789, Charles Thomson, Secretary of Congress, arrived at Mount Vernon to tell George Washington of his election. The question of whether Washington would serve was answered when he said, "I cannot give a greater evidence of my sensibility for the honor my fellow citizens have done me, than by accepting the appointment."

Washington left for New York on April 16. In his diary that day, he did not write about winning the election. Instead he wrote about his worries about doing the job well. He also wrote about his belief that he should serve "my country in obedience to its call."

His journey turned into a parade in every town where Washington was greeted enthusiastically with escorts, gun salutes, ringing of church bells, parades, speeches and ceremonial dinners. The people drew together in their trust and support of George Washington, and his journey came to symbolize their hopes for a transition to a new, unified government. He was inaugurated first president in New York City on April 30, 1789.

George Washington and Slavery

Many people wonder how George Washington, who has been called the father of liberty and freedom, could own slaves. By our modern social standards, it is hard to understand the world in which Washington lived – a world where human beings could be considered property and a world where slavery was common.

Washington at Mount Vernon

Although slavery had been a conventional practice in many parts of the world for thousands of years, chattel slavery - the system of slavery that developed in the North American colonies in the 17th and 18th centuries was particularly cruel. Under the laws of chattel slavery, slaves were considered property rather than people. In the eyes of the law, a slave had no greater legal standing than a horse or dog. Slaves could not legally own property. Their marriages were not recognized by law. Slaves could be bought, sold, and rented like any other form of property. They were given as gifts, bequeathed in wills, and even offered as prizes in lotteries

At the age of eleven, George Washington inherited ten slaves in his father's will. The institution of slavery had always been a part of his life – his father, brothers, and neighbors used slaves to work their land, serve in their homes, and help care for their children. As he grew older, Washington acquired additional slaves through purchase and through his marriage to Martha Dandridge Custis, a young widow who brought 25 slaves to Mount Vernon upon her marriage to Washington in 1759.

Washington kept over 3,000 acres under cultivation.

Many factors influenced Washington's use of slave labor at Mount Vernon during his lifetime, but the primary reason was a colonial plantation system that was dependent upon the availability of abundant labor. Washington and other large landowners kept thousands of acres under cultivation. From the earliest days of English settlement in the colonies, the issue of labor had been problematic. The colonies filled two roles in England's economy: they were a source of raw materials for its factories and people, and a market for finished goods. The colonies were; however, chronically short of laborers to produce the raw materials. In the 17th and early 18th centuries, colonists, particularly in Virginia, attempted to enslave Native Americans but quickly found that policy unsuccessful as the Native Americans could easily slip away and find refuge in their village or with other tribes. Although many laborers arrived in the colonies as indentured servants, their term of employment lasted from four to seven years, and the sheer amount of land under cultivation meant that there were too few indentured servants to meet the needs of large planters. Colonists began to look elsewhere for labor and the introduction of enslaved Africans became common in the colonies by the early 18th century. Economically, slavery was seemingly a better value for planters, as once a slave was purchased they were owned for life. Julian Neimcewicz, a Polish visitor to Mount Vernon in the late 18th century recorded his observations of slavery:

> *The real cause, or so it appears to me for the necessity and the existence of Negroes in the United States is the excessive extent of the individual properties, and the small number of whites that there are in view of the size of the country.*

George Washington had, since childhood, accepted the institution of slavery. For the last twenty-five years of his life, however, he struggled with the concept. As early as the 1770s, Washington decreed that he would no longer sell a slave without his or her permission because he was averse to breaking apart family units. Although the law did not recognize slave marriages, George Washington did recognize and encourage marriage in the community at Mount Vernon. His experience in the Revolution undoubtedly affected

Washington's perception of slavery as well, as evidenced as early as 1786 when he wrote to John Francis Mercer:

> *I never mean (unless some particular circumstances should compel me to it) to possess another slave by purchase; it being among my first wishes to see some plan adopted by the Legislature, by which slavery in the Country may be abolished by slow; sure and imperceptible degrees.*

He spent eight years leading the army – much of it in the North, where slavery was far less common than his native Virginia – and saw firsthand an economic system that did not depend upon the institution of slavery. Perhaps more importantly, the ideals for which he was fighting directly opposed a system that viewed human beings as property. It is almost certain that George Washington saw the irony in this situation. In 1794, he wrote to a friend;

> *Were it not then, that I am principled against selling Negroes, as you do cattle in the market, I would not, in twelve months, from this date, be possessed of one, as a slave.....*

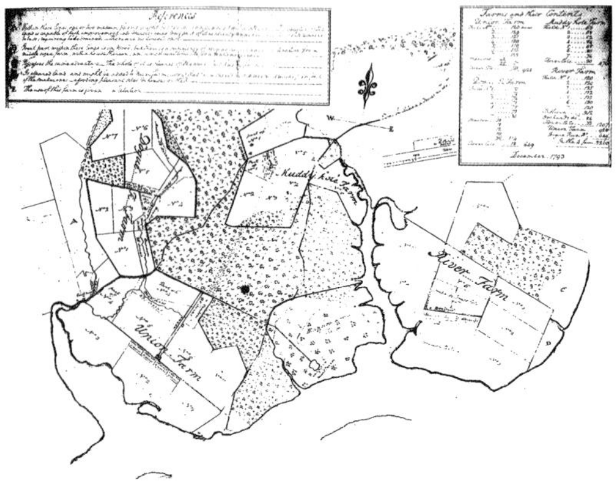

Map of Mount Vernon's five farms drawn by George Washington, 1793.

There was also a strong economic reason that factored heavily into Washington's changing attitude toward the use of slave labor. He was a very practical man, and both his calculation of the economic return on slaves and his experience at Mount Vernon made him question the economic viability of the system. At Mount Vernon, Washington was responsible for feeding and clothing a community of more than 300 people, almost one half of whom were either too old or too young to work.

In 1793, Washington actually developed a plan that he felt might allow him to free the Mount Vernon slaves. He wrote to British agriculturist Arthur Young and proposed renting all but the Mansion House Farm to British tenant farmers. Washington included a detailed map of his estate as well as a complete description of each farm. Part of his plan called for freeing the Mount Vernon slaves, who would then be paid a salary by the tenant farmers to work the land. His plans illustrate how deeply torn Washington had become over the issue of slavery. If successful, Washington would have been able to free his slaves and ensure they had a means of support. He feared that freeing slaves without providing them a proper training in a trade would set them adrift in the world. Washington never found any viable potential tenants, however and the plan was never implemented.

As president, Washington also faced the issue of slavery. On several occasions, he was approached by abolitionists who wanted his support to legally end the institution of slavery. Although his personal attitudes had changed, Washington feared the issue was volatile enough to tear the young nation apart. Believing that the southern states would never agree to abolition, he refused to take a public stand, fearing it could potentially generate a crisis in a government already struggling to establish policies agreeable to two new political parties. As president, he believed the abolition of slavery needed to be a legislative policy. As early as 1786, he wrote to a friend enlisting his support, *"there is not a man living who wishes more sincerely than I do, to see a plan adopted for the abolition of it [slavery]; but there is only one proper and effectual mode by which it can be accomplished, and that is by Legislative authority."*

Although he did not take a public stand, Washington chose to lead by example and used his will, which was later published, as a way to provide freedom for those slaves at Mount Vernon belonging to him. Of the 316 slaves living on the estate in 1799, 123 belonged to George Washington. Forty were rented, and the remainder were "dower" slaves belonging to the estate of Martha Washington's first husband. Upon his death, she, as his widow, had been given a lifetime interest in the property. By law, the Washington's were unable to free the "dower" slaves who legally belonged to Daniel Custis' other heirs. In his will, Washington made special provisions for Billy Lee, who had served him throughout the eight years of the Revolutionary War. Lee was freed immediately and provided with a pension of $30 per year. By the terms of his will, the remaining slaves were to be freed after Mrs. Washington's death. His will was quite specific:

> *Upon the decease of my wife, it is my Will and desire that all the Slaves which I hold in my own right shall receive their freedom....And I do hereby expressly forbid the Sale, or transportation out of said Commonwealth, of any Slave I may die possessed of, under any pretence whatsoever.*

Mrs. Washington chose not to wait to free the Washington slaves. Many historians theorize that, given the stipulations of Washington's will, she may have feared for her life, and on January 1, 1801, she legally freed George Washington's slaves. Their freedom for many, however, was tinged with sadness. Because so many of the slaves had intermarried with slaves from the Custis estate, families were broken apart as the "dower" slaves remained at Mount Vernon. After Mrs. Washington's death in 1802, they were divided among the Custis heirs as legal "property" that could be transferred from one person to another.

Slavery at Mount Vernon

Slaves at Mount Vernon lived and worked at all five farms and the gristmill. By 1799, 316 people, or 90% of the total Mount Vernon community were African American slaves. Of that number, 42% were either too old or too young to work or were disabled. By the time of Washington's death in 1799, the slave population consisted primarily of second and third generation individuals. Very few were actually natives of Africa, although Washington's step grandson, George Washington Parke Custis, wrote in his memoirs of "Father Jack," a slave born in Africa who would spend hours telling the young boy of his home country and how he was captured into slavery. Although Virginia law did not recognize slave marriages, George Washington encouraged marriage, and there were many family units at Mount Vernon, although husband and wife did not always live on the same farm. By law, children followed the condition of their mother. If the mother was a slave, then the child was a slave. If the mother were free, than her children were free. At Mount Vernon, if the mother were a "dower" slave, then her children were also "dower" slaves.

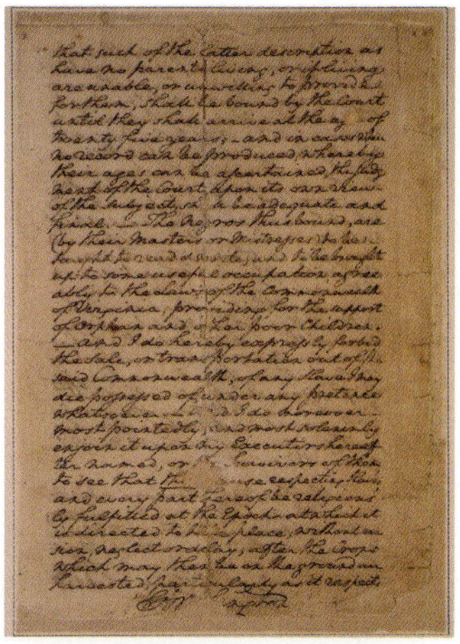

George Washington's will provided freedom for all slaves belonging to him.

Labor

Labor on the estate consisted of three main categories: skilled, domestic, and unskilled field workers. Domestic slaves worked in the Mansion and included both male and females. Skilled laborers such as coopers, spinners, blacksmiths, and carpenters were generally male, while most field workers were female. Of the total slave population at Mount Vernon, 75% were field workers, and of that number, 61% were adult women.

Until about the age of eleven, children looked after themselves and their younger siblings and performed such chores as getting water and hauling wood for their families. Between the ages of eleven and fourteen, children made up the transition group of "working boys and girls" who helped the adult work force in such tasks as making fences and hauling manure.

At Mount Vernon, the workweek for slaves was six days – Monday through Saturday – with Sundays off. The length of the workday changed with the different seasons. In the summer, when the sun rises at 5 o'clock in the morning and sets between 8 and 9 o'clock at night, the slaves were probably on the job for up to 15 or 16 hours a day. During the winter, however, the workday might have been as many as five or six hours shorter. Washington's papers show that the slaves were given two hours off during their workday for breakfast and dinner. In addition to Sundays off, the slaves at Mount Vernon received four days at Christmas, one day for Easter and another for Pentecost.

Adult women and men worked as field slaves at Mount Vernon.

Washington thought of himself first as a farmer, and even while away during the war and presidency, he kept in constant contact with his farm manager, who was required to submit a written weekly report. Although he maintained a formal relationship with the slaves at Mount Vernon, it is clear from his letters and instructions that he was very familiar with each – knowing their names, occupations, spouses, and children.

As a farmer, he was very intent on the work at his outlying farms where the production of crops took place. Routine jobs on the farms would have varied with the seasons. In the spring, people were busy with planting and caring for crops, following Washington's meticulous instructions for plowing, fertilizers, and crop rotation. The slaves worked in "gangs" comprised of eight to ten people, and they were assigned specific tasks such as hoer or plower. Each of the four outlying farms had slaves who lived and worked on the site, under an overseer who reported directly to the farm manager. Over the years Washington had several overseers who were slaves themselves. According to the 1799 census, the population at the farms was:

Dogue Run Farm – 45 slaves; 17 adult women; 7 adult men; 21 children

River Farm – 57 slaves; 23 adult women; 15 adult men; 19 children

Muddy Hole Farm – 42 slaves; 17 adult women; 7 adult men; 18 children

Union Farm – 72 slaves; 24 adult women; 18 adult men; 30 children

Many slaves also worked at one of Washington's three fisheries, which provided his most profitable industry. Several also lived and worked at the mill and distillery complex, which also housed his cooperage.

Harvesting of crops generally began in the summer and was completed in the fall, when pens were prepared to hold animals over the winter. During the winter months, crops were processed, seeds were saved, fences repaired, and hogs slaughtered and preserved for food.

Harvesting wheat

During the harvesting season, farm workers were joined by skilled and semi-skilled laborers from the Mansion House farm, gristmill, and other Mount Vernon farms. Everyone helped because the work had to be completed in a timely manner or the crops would be ruined. A system was developed during harvest with slaves assigned to such roles as cradlers, who cut the wheat; rakers, who gathered the wheat; shockers, who bound the wheat into sheaves; and conners, who stacked the sheaves before it was carted to a barn. It was not uncommon for slaves who worked hard during harvest to be granted a day off following the harvest of the crops.

The crops grown at Mount Vernon were used to feed the Washington family, the slave community, and livestock. The remainder was sold for profit.

Leisure Time

Although free time was limited for slaves living at Mount Vernon, it was not completely absent. Sundays were free from required work and many slaves spent the time attending to their own household chores, tending their gardens, telling stories, and playing music, games, and sports. Slaves were also allowed to hunt and fish to supplement their food rations. Washington sometimes issued guns for hunting, and two men, Tom Davis and Sambo Anderson, even sold duck they had hunted to Washington for use in the Mansion.

Visiting family and friends was another common use of free time. Often, family members lived on another of Mount Vernon's farms. They generally visited on Saturday nights, and "night walking" was a common occurrence as they traveled back and forth to visit at other farms or nearby properties. Washington, however, discouraged "night walking" on week-nights, believing that it made people too tired to work the next day. Many of the slaves kept their own gardens and raised poultry to sell at market in order to earn money for "luxuries." They were often allowed to go to the market in Alexandria to sell their goods and to shop at the merchants' stalls. Washington also allowed slaves to attend special events, as noted in his diary entry on October 9, 1786:

> *Allowed my People to go to the races in Alexandria on one of three days as best comported with their respective businesses.*

Slaves shared communal living quarters.

It is interesting to compare the lifestyles of the slaves living on outlying farms with those living on the Mansion House farm. Although those living at the Mansion House were generally the skilled workers and were accorded more privileges, they also lived in close proximity to the farm manager and the Washington family. Those living on outlying farms often had more freedom because of their distance from the central seat of the plantation and the farm manager. Although they worked long hours, they were not on constant call as were the cooks, maids, and butlers who worked directly for the family.

Living Quarters

There were three types of structures that housed slaves at Mount Vernon. The most permanent was a large two-story frame building with a brick foundation that stood at the Mansion House farm between 1760 and 1793. It was called the House for Families and housed almost 60 people who worked in and around the Mansion. The communal living space provided little privacy for slaves living there. The building was replaced by four large rooms in the wings of the new brick greenhouse Washington had built in the early 1790s. Small private quarters for skilled laborers were sometimes located in the buildings where they worked, such as the blacksmiths shop or kitchen. Finally, field workers lived in small log structures daubed with mud. One can imagine the impermanence and quality of these homes by reading a letter written by George Washington to his farm manager in 1793:

The original greenhouse slave quarters were built in 1793.

> *Removing the largest kind of Negro quarters (the smaller ones or cabbins I presume the people with little assistance of Carts can do themselves) to the ground marked out for them....*

The houses were very crude by our standards today, with very little furniture and few personal belongings. There was seldom privacy and the buildings were most likely dirty and smoky. Rodents were a constant problem, and many slaves kept cats or dogs to help control them. In 1798, Julian Niemcewicz, a Polish visitor to Mount Vernon visited one of the outlying farms. In his diary he described a home he visited:

This cabin is believed to be one of the original outlying slave cabins at Mount Vernon.

> *We entered one of the huts of the Blacks, for one can not call them by the name of Houses. They are more miserable than the most miserable of the cottages of our peasants. The husband and wife sleep on a mean pallet, the children on the ground; a very bad fireplace, some utensils for cooking, but in the middle of this poverty some cups and a teapot.*

Although the quarters of slaves living on the Mansion House farm were more substantial and comfortable, they, too, provided little privacy and were located close to the Mansion where the slaves were always on call.

Health problems were often made worse by close quarters. Slaves suffered from fleas, intestinal parasites, and body mites. Children were especially susceptible to respiratory and intestinal problems and frequently suffered accidents. Dr. James Craik, who had served with Washington in the war and remained his personal physician, was called to the plantation to treat serious medical problems among the slaves.

Clothing

Clothing was issued once a year and supplemented seasonally. Much of the cloth used for clothing the slaves was manufactured at Mount Vernon, although records show that Washington did order Osnabrig (a coarse linen) from Europe.

Men received breeches of wool and linen, a short wool jacket, 2 Osnabrig shirts, one pair of stockings and one pair of shoes. Women were given two Osnabrig shifts, a petticoat (skirt), a short gown (jacket) with fitted bodice, one pair of stockings, and one pair of shoes. One new blanket was distributed each year as well. The clothing was plain and coarse, with the exception of house servants who were issued formal livery. They and the most productive workers were given a better quality of clothing, while the poorest quality was given to children, the old, and the disabled.

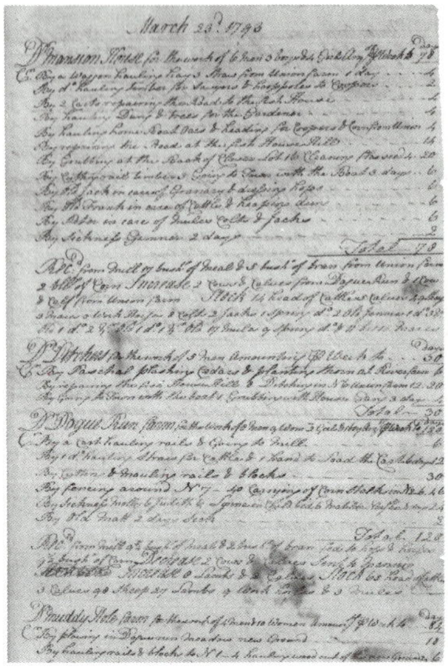
March 23d 1793

Weekly work report submitted to George Washington.

Food

Food rations were distributed weekly. Each working slave received a peck of cornmeal (eight quarts), salted fish, buttermilk, and some meat, usually lesser quality cuts than those served in the Mansion. Food was also used as a reward for good work and extra rations were given during the busy harvest season as well. And, many slaves kept gardens for fresh vegetables and raised fowl for meat and eggs to supplement their diet. Archaeological excavations at the House for Families slave quarters in 1990 provided a tremendous amount of information about the diet of slaves living at Mount Vernon. The excavation of over 25,000 bones, for example, revealed that the slaves living in the quarters had a much more varied diet than previously believed.

The House for Families Slave Quarter

Investigating History

Today, most Americans learn about George Washington in school. But in order to understand his home, Mount Vernon, as a community and as a business, it is necessary to learn about Tom Davis, Kitty, Doll, Frank, Nat, and the other slaves who lived there in the 1700s. Washington was a meticulous record keeper - his letters will fill more than 90 volumes when editing is completed. In addition, invoices, weekly work reports, newspapers, and censuses provide detailed information for historians investigating the daily life of both the Washington family and the slave community. These primary documents provide tremendous detail. What is missing, however, from the study of these documents? For the large part they were written by George Washington, his family, his overseers, farm managers, or visitors to Mount Vernon and represent their perspective of events and people. Very few slaves were trained to read or write and, therefore, there is very little existing primary documentation that reveals their views, personalities, or opinions.

Archaeological excavation on the site of the House for Families.

How then do we learn about the lives of people whose lives may have been controlled under the institution of slavery, but whose thoughts, dreams, and hopes were their own? Archaeological investigation has played an integral role in exploring the entire Mount Vernon community. In addition to the excavation of sites associated with the Washington family, such as the Mansion kitchen midden, Mount Vernon archaeologists have excavated several sites where slaves lived and worked. Perhaps the most significant excavation took place at the House for Families Slave quarters located a short distance from the Mansion. Approximately 60 people lived in the communal quarter. They knew little or no privacy in their daily lives. The excavation of their home provided a more intimate glimpse into their lives than previously revealed through documents. While the enormous amount of primary documents available to historians tell us details such as the slaves' names, occupations, ages and relationships – they fail to record their point of view. Archaeology allows their story to be told through personal possessions; the 65,000 artifacts excavated from the site offer a tangible link to the slaves themselves.

Archaeological investigation uncovered ornaments such as buckles (top left), fine ceramics (top right), lead shot and flint (botom left), and over 25,000 animal bones (bottom right).

The excavation at the House for Families opened a door into understanding personal lives – allowing us to see what the slaves ate, the plates and glasses they used, how they entertained themselves, how they decorated their clothing, and the tools they used. Over 25,000 animals bones disclosed that the diet of the slave community was much more varied than previously believed. Archaeology revealed that their diet included a variety of fish, oyster, turkey, duck, chicken, deer, squirrel, pork, beef, sheep, and opossum. Archaeologists also uncovered a surprising amount of finer glasswares and ceramics, leading to the theory that once a piece was damaged or went out of fashion it was passed from the Mansion to the slave quarters. Most of the slaves living in the quarter worked in and around the Mansion and had daily contact with the family. In addition, the discovery of tools helped determine the occupations of slaves living in the quarter. They may have also used tools for use in their own gardens. Buttons, watch fobs, and jewelry helped illustrate personal adornment. The excavation of lead shot and gunflint reinforced primary document evidence that slaves were issued guns by Washington to hunt. Clay pipe fragments, jaw harps, and game pieces helped reveal leisure time activities of people living in the quarters. The excavations at the House For Families offered a unique look into the lives of people living there more than 200 years ago. While we can never fully understand what is was like to be enslaved, archaeology at Mount Vernon has played an important role in providing insight into a community of more than 300 people who lived and worked at Mount Vernon as slaves.

Rebellion

At Mount Vernon, and other plantations where large numbers of African Americans were viewed as property, it was not uncommon for those enslaved against their will to express their sense of freedom and individuality through non-threatening methods of rebellion. Misplacing or breaking tools, work stoppage, illness, and even theft were common forms of passive rebellion. There was little a slave owner could do to curtail this form or rebellion, and it is clear from Washington's papers that he often suspected the enslaved people at Mount Vernon of neglecting their work, of suspicious illnesses, or of theft. Consider correspondence written by Washington to his farm manager, William Pearce:

January 1794

> *Speaking of these Seeds, I must give you a hint of what I also very strongly suspect; - and that is – that my Negro Seedsmen take a considerable toll from every thing that goes into their hands – for that reason, make it an invariable rule before it is delivered to them, to mix in a bushel of Sand or well dried earth, as many pints of seed as you allow to an Acre, and let it be sown in this manner......in this State, the Seed is rendered unsaleable.....*

I find by the Reports that Sam is, in a manner, always returned sick; - Doll at the Ferry, and several of the Spinners very frequently so, for a week at a stretch; and Ditcher Charles often laid up with a lameness. – I never wish my people to work when they are really sick, or unfit for it; on the contrary, that all necessary care should be taken of them when they are so; - but if you do not examine into their complaints, they will lay by when no more ails them than ails those who stick to their business.....

December 1794:

I perceive by the Spinning report of last week, that each of the spinners have deducted half a pound for dirty wool. – to avoid this in the future (for if left to themselves they will soon deduct a pound, or more) it would be best to let them receive none but clean wool.

(Washington always expected a minimum of five pounds of clean wool from his sheep. He often believed that slaves were taking wool for their own use)

February 1795:

The tedious manner in which my carpenters seem to execute every thing they take in hand, is extremely to be regretted. – They seem from the reports, to have been weeks getting scantling for the Sheds at D: Run; when, from the idea I had of this work, I presumed a few days would have sufficed..... Two weeks later he wrote again regarding the carpenters, *...In short, it appears to me, that to make even a chicken coop, would employ all of them a week; - buildings that are run up here in two or three days (with not more hands) employ them a month, or more.*

June 1795

I wish you could find out the thief who robbed the Meat house at Mount Vernon, and bring him to punishment......Nathan has been suspected, if not detected, in an attempt of this sort formerly; and is as likely as any one to be guilty of it now. – Postilion Joe has been caught in similar practices; - and Sam, I am sure would not be restrained by any qualms of conscience.

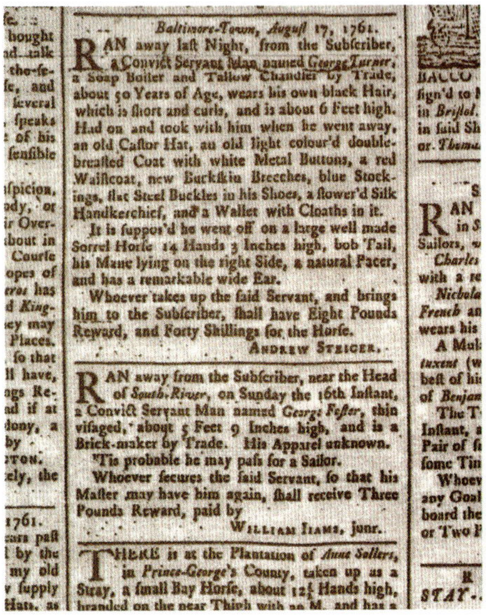
Baltimore-Town, August 17, 1761.

RAN away last Night, from the Subscriber, a Convict Servant Man named George Turner, a Soap Boiler and Tallow Chandler by Trade, about 50 Years of Age, wears his own black Hair, which is short and curls, and is about 6 Feet high. Had on and took with him when he went away, an old Castor Hat, an old light colour'd double-breasted Coat with white Metal Buttons, a red Waistcoat, new Buckskin Breeches, blue Stockings, flat Steel Buckles in his Shoes, a flower'd Silk Handkerchief, and a Wallet with Cloaths in it.

It is suppos'd he went off on a large well made Sorrel Horse 14 Hands 3 Inches high, bob Tail, his Mane lying on the right Side, a natural Pacer, and has a remarkable wide Ear.

Whoever takes up the said Servant, and brings him to the Subscriber, shall have Eight Pounds Reward, and Forty Shillings for the Horse.

ANDREW STEIGER.

RAN away from the Subscriber, near the Head of South-River, on Sunday the 16th Instant, a Convict Servant Man named George Foster, thin visaged, about 5 Feet 9 Inches high, and is a Brick-maker by Trade. His Apparel unknown.

'Tis probable he may pass for a Sailor.

Whoever secures the said Servant, so that his Master may have him again, shall receive Three Pounds Reward, paid by

WILLIAM IIAMS, junr.

THERE is at the Plantation of Anne Sellers, in Prince-George's County, taken up as a Stray, a small Bay Horse, about 12½ Hands high,

Runaway slave ads were commonly placed in local newspapers.

July 1795

Davy's lost lambs, carry with them a very suspicious appearance; ....If the lambs has been poisoned, or had died a natural death...their bones would have been forth coming, and his not being able to produce them is an argument both of his guilt, and of his not expecting to be called upon for that evidence......

(Davy was a slave overseer whom Washington generally thought highly of. In this case he suspected that Davy might be protecting "very sly and cunning rogues" who had sold the lambs)

August 1795

A sett of Ploughs, made and taken care of as they ought to be, canot, surely want replacing as often as mine are.....

February 1796

I see by the last weeks report that Caesar has been absent six days. – Is he a runaway? If so, it is probable he will escape all together as he can read, if not write. –

While his attitude towards his slaves may seem exacting, Washington's correspondence from the war and to his overseers and farm managers reflects a very similar attitude towards his soldiers, hired assistants, and contemporaries, as well. It was very much in line with the way George Washington perceived the concepts of labor and duty. A slave, freed by Washington in his will, perhaps summed up George Washington's attitude most clearly, writing in 1838:

> *The sun never caught him [Washington] in bed, and he was unwilling it should find any of his people sleeping.*

Conclusion

George Washington was a relatively typical slave owner of his time. He differed from many of his contemporaries by recognizing the rights of people to marry, by his refusal to break apart family units, and by his general unwillingness to exert corporal punishment except in what he viewed as extreme cases of misconduct. However, like his contemporaries he, for much of his life, accepted the institution of slavery. But, one of the most remarkable aspects of George Washington's character was his life-long quest to educate himself. His ideas, perceptions, and actions reflected his study of new theories in agriculture, of the study of military strategy, of constitutional and republican ideals, and, it is fair to say, his view of the institution of slavery. Just as his actions in leading the army, in leading the government, and in pioneering new methods of farming changed and evolved, Washington came to view slavery as an unacceptable institution. Although he was conscious of the fact that his actions would not end slavery in the nation, or present an "ideal" solution to the issue of slavery, he took steps through his personal actions and through his will to express his belief that the institution of slavery should gradually be abolished in the United States.

Discussion Topics

1. Discuss George Washington's attitude towards slavery when he was young and when he was older. What do your students think changed his attitude? Do your students think it was unusual for George Washington to have provided for the freedom of slaves in his will?
2. Discuss how laws and society change over time. Is this good or bad? Are there any things we do today that our grandchildren might think of as wrong?
3. Discuss the operation of an 18th-century plantation. What do your students think were the roles of the owner, the overseers, the indentured servants, and the slaves?
4. Discuss the roles of skilled slaves and unskilled field workers. What were the advantages for each of these groups?
5. Discuss the idea of passive rebellion with your students. Was it wrong for slaves to express their individuality and freedom in this way? What other ways might a person rebel without violence?

George Washington In Art

Art is a valuable tool with which to teach the past. It offers a unique record of history, can reveal the way people lived and thought in a certain period, and provides a tangible reflection of a society's history and cultural mores. Before photography was invented in the mid-19th century, people relied on artists to relay important events, to teach history, to tell stories, and to honor and remember heroes.

Today, we all see an image of George Washington on a daily basis when we pay for movie tickets, buy groceries, shop for clothes and use the dollar bill as payment. It is an image that is engrained, whether we realize it or not, in our memories and shapes the way we perceive or remember our nation's first president. For more than 150 years following his death, however, Washington was immortalized in a wide variety of images -- images that displayed him as a heroic military hero, as a wise and strong president, as a loving family man, and as a symbol of the nation. Over 30 different artists painted Washington during his life time. He did not enjoy sitting for portraits - *"I am so hackneyed to the touches of the Painters pencil, that I am now altogether at their beck, and sit like patience on a Monument whilst they are delineating the lines of my face..."* - however, he did it because there was tremendous demand for his image. Paintings were commissioned as gifts, for admirers, for display in public areas, and as personal mementos. Often, artists would paint many copies of a popular work, and later the images were mass-produced to meet the vast public demand through lithographs and engravings. As his fame grew, the demand for his image spread to Europe. Before the days of cameras and electronic media, however, Europeans had no way of knowing what Washington looked like. But there was still a large market for his image and artists on the continent began to create fictionalized images of the American hero that proved very popular with his admirers overseas.

Textbooks traditionally cover the facts of George Washington's accomplishments. This chapter is intended to help your students understand the power of the image and how art reflects the opinions and beliefs of society. Two hundred years ago, there was perhaps no more powerful and immediately recognizable image than that of George Washington.

Getting Started

Have your students discuss the fact that throughout time, art has been a way to record history. From early cave art to modern times, artists have painted scenes that tell stories of historical events. Before the invention of photography, artists were also hired to paint individuals and families, much as we would have a family photograph taken today. These paintings tell us a great deal about life in the past. Ask your students how they record events in their family today. Have they ever been part of a formal family or school photograph? Of an informal photograph taken at a picnic, game, family gathering, or school? What do they do with their photographs? Could someone looking at the photographs learn anything about the student's life?

Ask your students to consider the idea that when looking at historical paintings we are seeing events or ideas through the eyes of the person who painted the picture. Often, the images reflect the belief and ideals of the people who lived in that time. In the 18th and 19th centuries, many images were meant to inspire pride in one's country and a feeling of patriotism. As commander in chief of the Continental Army, president of the Constitutional Convention, and first president of the United States, George Washington remained one of the defining symbols of the nation for more than 150 years.

In the late 18th century and throughout the 19th century, lithographs and engravings were mass-produced and widely sold. Because they were easy to produce, lithographs and engravings offered many people access to art; providing the average American with affordable copies of famous artworks or portraits. The subjects of these images in many ways reflected the attitudes, beliefs, and tastes of Americans. George Washington was one of the most popularly sold images of the period - not only in the United States, but in Europe as well. Hundreds of images of Washington were created and sold for people to hang in their homes, businesses, and schools. Ask your students if they have posters (or have at one time decorated their room with posters). Discuss the idea that posters are the 20th century equivalent of 19th-century lithographs and engravings. What kinds of posters are popular today - landscapes, sports heroes, movie stars, politicians? How do they reflect popular culture?

Types of Pictures

PORTRAIT: Portraits may be of one person or of a group. They may show the person in full length, just the head and shoulders, or just the head. There may be objects in the picture related to the character and personality of the person or to an important event in his or her life. Look at *G. Washington*. This engraving is perhaps the best known image of George Washington and the one readily identified by most people. Gilbert Stuart painted the original for the Boston Athenaeum in 1796 at the end of Washington's presidency. There is no story in this picture, no symbolism, no military celebration, nor any presidential moment. Rather, Stuart simply represented a carefully observed image of a noble and dignified man.

Many prints and paintings were made of George Washington in the 18th century. He sat for more than 30 different artists, including painters and sculptors. The most accurate likenesses of Washington are paintings that were drawn from actual sittings, like the Athenaeum painting, of which this engraving is an accurate copy. The Athenaeum portrait is perhaps the most copied portrait of Washington. Its popularity made George Washington instantly recognizable in the United States.

HISTORY PAINTINGS: These paintings record important events and often contain easily identifiable symbols and people. In studying history paintings, such as the *Battle of Princeton*, we see that artists often fictionalized or amplified aspects of an event. In many cases they were making up for a lack of first hand information, the artist was attempting to improve or dramatize the scene, or stressing a point of view. In many cases also, the goal of the artist was to stress the idea of George Washington, not to present accurate historic details. It is important to remember that the artists of the 19th century were painting with different historical information and different perspectives than late 20th century views. Have your students think about when these pictures were made and what that may signify.

GENRE is another popular image type. Portraits of George Washington did not always show him as a military hero or as the president. Sometimes they showed him as an ordinary man, performing an ordinary task. Genre pictures generally depict a scene of figures relaxing or working. They are "slice of life" images, or simple moments in time captured by the artist.

Discussion Topics and Suggested Activities

1. Ask each student to bring in an image from a newspaper, magazine, or family photo album. Have each student write a brief label describing how their image relates information or tells a story. Review the images as a group. Discuss whether images can be "staged" or dramatized to heighten a point of view. Do photographers use light, perspective, or tension to set a mood or tell a story? How?

2. Create a collage of images focusing on a current national figure. Ask your students if the images can be used to tell a story or present a point of view. How might their collage be analyzed or viewed by people two hundred years in the future? Will people in the future will have the same view of the events or person the students have selected?

3. Using the list your students created of George Washington's accomplishments and personal characteristics, discuss how they would portray those ideas in art. Do they think their images would look different from paintings of the 18th and 19th centuries? Why?

4. Have your students compare one image of George Washington from this lesson with a poster of a modern hero. How are two images similar? Different? What do they think the purpose of the images are? Next, ask your students to create a diary entry, newspaper article, or other first person account telling a story about one of the images they have selected.

Look at *The Home of Washington.* This genre picture attempts to describe George Washington in his domestic roles as friend, husband, grandfather, and plantation manager, after the war, but before he became president. The Marquis de Lafayette visited Mount Vernon in 1784, a few years after the Revolutionary War. Lafayette and Washington here appear to be discussing some current event, perhaps, in a serene, pleasant setting.

Examining Elements in Art

The artist is a manipulator of the eye. Without our realizing it, he makes us look in specific places in the picture, in a certain order, by his use of composition or arrangement of elements. As you look at the pictures in this chapter, notice the direction of lines and repeated patterns of light, color, and figures.

How are artistic elements used to tell a story or enhance an image? Within each picture there are different elements that work together to create the composition and an appealing picture. Perspective can give the picture a sense of space and dimension. Look at *Washington Taking Command of the American Army.* Notice that the soldiers standing at attention in a long, straight line appear to become progressively smaller and to disappear into the far distance near the tents. This use of diminishing perspective gives us a feeling of being in a large open space. Atmospheric perspective makes objects in the distance seem farther away by fading and blurring them.

Sometimes the space in a picture is shallow, as in *Inauguration of Washington.* The room appears small, and all the figures are standing more or less on the same plane. The shallow space in this picture creates a sense of intimacy.

Light is another important element of art. The artist may depict natural daylight, moonlight, candlelight, or even light from an unknown source. Light can change the way one interprets a picture by creating an emotional effect. An artist may also use light to emphasize faces or other important parts of the picture. The arrangement of the brighter and darker areas in a picture can help to guide our eyes through the scene. Look at the light in *Washington Crossing the Delaware.* This scene shows General George Washington leading the American troops across the Delaware River under cover of night to Trenton, New Jersey, where they defeated the British the next day, December 26th, 1776. The circular field of light centered over Washington conveys confidence, and it may even be read as a heavenly, guiding light. The light also creates a silhouette, making Washington stand apart from the crowd.

The use of line, shapes and patterns is another aspect of composition that can guide the viewer through the picture. A good example of this is in *The Life of George Washington: The Farmer.* Even though the title suggests that Washington is the subject, we know he is not the main focus because the lines of the composition point away from him. Begin looking on the right, where Washington is standing. The riding crop in his hand points to a figure bending over. The standing figure in the center is holding a sickle in his left hand that leads to the male and female figures next to him. If you begin looking from the left, you see that the man on the wagon has a long pole that also points to this group of three central figures. The composition is telling us that the three central slave figures are the real subject of this picture.

Another use of line is to create tension. In *Washington Crossing the Allegheny,* 21-year old Washington and his guide, Christopher Gist, are shown on the raft that they built on December 29, 1753, to cross the semi-frozen Allegheny River. It is a dramatic scene, and the artist enhanced the sense of tension by using opposing diagonal lines. The strong lines of the rafters' setting poles are diagonal to the picture plane. The lines of the men's bodies are at an opposing diagonal. Notice how in calm or static pictures, horizontal lines predominate.

A common artistic technique employed by artists of the 18th and 19th century was the use of symbolism to relate a concept or an abstract ideal. Artists shared a lexicon of symbols. Well known symbols included the olive branch representing peace, the female figure of "Liberty" wearing the liberty cap and often holding a sword, the feminine "Justice" holding the scales of justice, the cornucopia, or horn of plenty, emblematic of prosperity and the weeping willow representing death or mourning.

After his death in December 1799, Washington was buried in the family vault at Mount Vernon. Following directions left in his will, a new tomb was built in 1831, shown here in *Mount-Vernon, Tomb of Washington*. Washington's tomb became a pilgrimage site to those wishing to pay respects to the great leader. In this image, you will note that the artist has used several symbols to relate themes or ideas. The small, dead tree in the center could represent Washington's untimely death; the dog might represent the loyal faith of Americans to the father of their country; the river may represent a passage; and the water may also be read as a purifying element.

Discussion Topics and Suggested Activities

1. Ask your students to find an image in which the artist or photographer uses light to enhance the scene or set a mood. They should write a brief description of how the use of light affects the message of the picture they have chosen.

2. Work with your school's art teacher and have your students draw an image using lines to show perspective and tension and to set the composition of their image.

3. Discuss the use of symbolism in art. Next, have each student select a character trait they believe George Washington represents. Then ask them to create a symbol they believe would represent this trait in art.

ELEMENTS IN ART

Lines: The artist uses diagonal and opposing lines to convey tension. See how the lines of the bayonets in the foreground and background are opposing. Washington's sword is pointing in an opposite direction from the way he is facing. This opposition conveys motion and tension. Washington's horse is partly rearing and his posture suggests that Washington is controlling him.

Composition: The artist uses objects to create a circle around Washington. One can draw a line from object to object - soldiers to tree trunk, to column, to building, to soldiers, leaving Washington as the central figure in this circular imagery.

Symbolism: While the artist does not employ overt symbols, the central figure of General Washington holding his sword and ready for battle represents America's struggle for liberty, in effect making Washington himself a symbol.

Perspective: Notice how the line of troops diminishes in size from the right foreground to the center background (linear perspective). The background elements also appear to recede because the artist has evened their tone and blurred their edges (atmospheric perspective).

Light: Look how the artist has made the main light source appear to reflect from the snow. This bright foreground light contrasts with the subdued sky in the background. The placement of Washington alone on the illuminated surface of the snow enhances his role as the central figure in the composition.

***Washington Crossing the Delaware*.**
Engraved by Paul Giradet, after painting by Emanuel Leutze.
Published by Goupil & Col., New York, 1853.

The Life of George Washington: The Farmer

Lithograph by Claude Regnier, after painting by Junius Brutus Stearns.

Published by M. Knoedler, New York, 1853.

The Home of Washington.

Engraving by Thomas Oldham Barlow, after painting by Thomas Prichard Rossiter and Louis Remy Mignot.

1860.

The Washington Family.
Engraver unknown, after painting by Edward Savage, mid-19th century.

DISCUSSION QUESTIONS

Break your students into four groups. Assign each group one of the 8 1/2 x 11 images provided in this chapter. The images are on perforated pages and can be laminated. Return the images to the pockets provided in the book at the completion of this activity. As your students examine the images, have them consider the following questions:

1. Title: ______________________ Artist: ______________________

   What is portrayed in the picture? Does the picture tell a story?

2. How does the picture make you feel?

3. Do you think the picture is historically correct? Why or why not?

4. Does the artist use symbols? If you answer yes, what symbols are used and what do you think they represent?

   What symbols would you use to tell the same story?

5. Does the artist use any of the following techniques:

   A. Light ____ B. Tension ____ C. Lines ____ D. Perspective ___

   If you answer yes, how does the artist use these elements to tell a story? Do you think these elements in art help make the image dramatic or real? Why?

6. What does the image tell you about George Washington? Does the picture make him heroic? Why or why not?

Learning Through Primary Source Documents

In this chapter, you will find four primary source documents provided to help your students analyze George Washington, his contributions to the founding of our nation, and life on his 18th-century estate, Mount Vernon. Each document includes a description that provides background and context for use and discussion in the classroom. Through primary document research, your students will gain experience in examining original primary source materials, comparing and contrasting evidence from different sources, the analysis of data and formulating hypothesis based on written evidence, and gain a deeper understanding of George Washington and 18th-century life.

We suggest that prior to using the documents with your students you review the primary source materials. Explain to the students that primary source documents were created by people who have firsthand knowledge of historical events. Before beginning the lesson, ask your students to create a list of what they believe could be defined as primary sources. The list can include letters, diaries, newspapers, photographs or paintings, maps, censuses, objects or artifacts, video documentaries, and other first hand materials. Discuss the idea that primary sources almost always reflect the opinion, memory, or bias of the creator.

Primary sources, perhaps most importantly, provide students with a real link to people who lived in the past. The study of primary sources opens a door to a personal connection with history and allows students the stimulation of connecting with actual people and events through their own words and observations. In this section, your students will have the opportunity to explore the character and personality of a man whose deeds, words, and images were the raw material of both great history and fascinating myth.

It is estimated that George Washington wrote over 40,000 letters in his lifetime. In addition, he kept a daily diary from the time that he was a young boy. He also kept meticulous records of invoices, farm reports and other business calculations. Mount Vernon is perhaps the best-documented Chesapeake plantation in existence today. That documentation helps historians greatly and, more importantly; his diaries and letters reveal George Washington's personality and beliefs more clearly than any second hand source can.

Documents:

Excerpt, My Journey Over the Mountains, 1747

Mission to the Ohio, Map Drawn by George Washington, 1753

The Massachusetts Gazette, March 13, 1787

Census of Slaves at Mount Vernon, 1799

Discussion Topics

1. Discuss with your students the process of communication in the 18th century. Today, we use the telephone or e-mail to communicate with friends and family. Two hundred years ago, communication was done by letter. If the students had to write a letter every time they wanted to share news with a friend, how many letters would they write in the next year?

Excerpts From the Journals of George Washington

The first of George Washington's journals that still exists is one which he began at age 16. He continued to keep journals with some regularity for the remainder of his life. The following excerpts are from three journals. The spelling, abbreviations, and capitalization are Washington's throughout. Brackets indicate modern additions or explanations.

Surveying trip with George Fairfax at age 16

A Journal of my Journey over the Mountains began Fryday the 11th of March 1747/8. Tuesday 15th. We set out early with Intent to Run round the sd. [said-mentioned in previous entry] Land but being taken in a Rain &it Increasing very fast obliged us to return. It clearing about one oClock & our time being too Precious to Loose we a second time ventured out & Worked hard till Night & then returned to Penningtons we got our Suppers & was Lighted in to a Room & I not being so good a Woodsman as the rest of my Company striped my self very orderly & went in to the Bed as they call'd it when to my Surprize I found it to be nothing but a Little Straw-Matted together without Sheets or any thing else but only one Thread Bear blanket with double its Weight of Vermin such as Lice Fleas & c. Had we not have been very tired, I am sure we should not have slep'd much that night. I made a Promise not to Sleep so from that time forward chusing rather to sleep in the open Air before a fire as will Appear hereafter.

April 1760-Farm Experiments at Mount Vernon

Monday Apl. 14. Fine warm day, Wind So[uther]ly and clear till the eveng. when it clouded. No Fish were to catchd to day neither. Mixd my Composts in a box with ten Apartments in the following manner viz. [namely]- in No. 1 is three pecks of the Earth brought from below the Hill out of the 46 Acre Field without any mixture- in No. 2 is two pecks of the said Earth and one of Marle taken out of the said Field which Marle seemd a little Inclinable to Sand. 3. Has 2 Pecks of sd. Earth and 1 of Riverside Sand. 4. Has a Peck of Horse Dung. 5. Has Mud taken out of the Creek. 6. Has Cow Dung. 7. Marle from the Gullys on the Hill side wch. seemd to be purer than the other. 8. Sheep Dung. 9. Black Mould taken out of the Pocoson on the Creek side. 10. Clay got just below the Garden. All mixd with the same quantity & sort of Earth in the most effectual manner by reducing the whole to a tolerable degree of fineness & jubling them well together in a Cloth. In each of these divisions were planted three Grains of Wheat 3 of Oats & as many of Barley, all at equal distances in Rows & of equal depth (done by a Machine made for the purpose)....Two or three hours after sowing in this manner, and about an hour before Sun set I watered them all equally alike with Water that had been standing in a Tub abt. two hours exposed to the Sun.

April, 16 1789—Inaugural journey

About 10 Oclock I bade adieu to Mount Vernon, to private life, and to domestic felicity, and with a mind oppressed with more anxious and painful sensations than I have words to express, set out for New York in company with Mr. Thompson, and Colonel Humphries, with the best dispositions to render service to my country in obedience to its call, but with less hope of answering its expectations.

Suggested Activities

1. Have each student keep his or her own journal for a week. Afterwards, invite them to discuss and compare their journals. Did the students record what they did or what they thought? Are their entries on weekdays different from those on weekends?

2. Have your students plan a trip. Address the following: the purpose, destination and length of the trip, the mode of transportation, the weather and time of year, the people traveling, the people being left behind. How will a trip today differ from one in Washington's time?

and sold by James Wood prior to this. Lord Fairfax shortly after this date made an addition to the town, and donated the ground for an Episcopal church. Frederick county early took measures to give protection to its settlers by building forts, making roads and establishing ferries. Its productive soil at the same time bountifully rewarded the husbandman for his labor. As the Frederick county courts were held at Winchester, the people adopted the southern habit of calling the place where the courts met by the name of the county, thus it was frequently spoken of as Frederick Town and is so designated in several of the early maps. Fort Loudoun was erected here by direction of the Assembly of Virginia in 1756, under the immediate supervision of Major Washington.

[13] Cate's marsh and Long marsh — these are names of small streams which flow from the foot hill of North mountain to the Shenandoah river and have along their course considerable meadow or marshy land. Long marsh is of sufficient importance to be named upon the maps of Virginia.

Tuesday 15th We set out early with Intent to Run round ye sd Land but being taken in a Rain & it Increasing very fast obliged us to return, it clearing about one oClock & our time being too Precious to Loose we a second time ventured out & Worked hard till Night & then return'd to Penningtons we got our Suppers & was Lighted into a Room & I not being so good a Woodsman as ye rest of my Company striped myself very orderly & went in to ye Bed as they called it when to my Surprize I found it to be nothing but a Little Straw — Matted together without Sheets or any thing else but only one thread Bear blanket with double its Weight of Vermin such as Lice Fleas &c[14] I was glad to get up (as soon as y

[14] For comments on fleas and other vermin see note 4. Washington's "Rules of Civility and Decent Behaviour," p. 14,

Washington's association with frontiersmen in their primitive cabins, which the position of a surveyor in the then almost unbroken forest necessitated, was to him a new and peculiar experience. His observations and reflections of the first few days are recorded with a naivete which is truly charming.

Light was carried from us) I put on my Cloths & Lays as my Companions. Had we not have been very tired I am sure we should not have slep'd much that night I made a Promise not to Sleep so from that time forward chusing rather to sleep in y. open Air before a fire as will appear hereafter.

March y. 15th 1747–8 Survey'd for George Fairfax Esqr. a Tract of Land lying on Cates Marsh and Long Marsh Begining at three Red Oaks Fx on a Ridge the No Side a Spring Branch being corner to ye 623 Acre Tract & Extending thence No 30° Et 436 poles to a Large Hickory and Red Oak Fx near John Cozines house thence No 60° Wt 90 Poles to a Large White Oak Fx thence No 7° Et 365 poles to Long Marsh 420 poles to 2 Red Oaks and W: Oak in a Poyson'd field[15] by a

[15] This probably has reference to some pernicious weeds unfavorable to tillage and injurious to grazing animals, as St. John's wort. Farmers believe that this, and certain other noxious weeds which occasionally invade pasture fields, cause sore mouths and legs in horses and horned cattle and affect the milk of cows grazing where it grows.

Road thence No 65° Wt 134 Poles to a W: Oak by ye sd Marsh thence crossing ye Marsh So 20° Wt 126 poles to another Branch: of Long Marsh 218 poles to a Red Oak Fx thence No 80° Wt 558 po: to a Large Red Oak & White Oak Fx in a Valley thence S

Excerpt, My Journey Over the Mountains

In 1747 George Washington accompanied George William Fairfax on a surveying trip to the Shenandoah Valley area of Virginia, which was then the western frontier. Washington was only 16 years old and the trip was an adventure. It also helped him learn the skill of surveying, which became his first career. Through this trip, George Washington gained a life-long love and knowledge of the frontier. He kept a diary of his entire trip and this became a practice for the rest of his life. Historians know a great deal about George Washington by reading his diaries. This diary was originally published in 1892 by Joel Munsell's Sons in Albany, New York. You can read comments from the editor on the page.

Suggested Activities

1. George Washington was largely self-educated. His formal schooling ended when he was just 15 years old. When he was older, he went back and corrected the spelling and grammar in many of his early writings. After reading the diary entry make a chart with two columns. In the first column list any word that is misspelled. In the second column, write the correct spelling of the word.

2. George Washington was not an experienced woodsman on his first trip to the frontier. What story does he tell in his diary that lets you know he had not traveled and slept in frontier inns before his trip in 1747?

3. George Washington's trip to the frontier was his first experience surveying. Within two years, he had become a very successful surveyor. The common measurement for surveying 200 years ago was two poles, which equals 33 feet. Read the entry for March 15. Based on calculation of two poles = 33 feet, determine the distances between the landmarks Washington uses. Why do you think he uses trees as boundary markers?

4. George Washington kept a diary for most of his life. Keep a journal for one week. In your journal you should record your daily activities, any places you visit, how long your journey took, and any people you meet. At the end of a week, compare your journal with those of your classmates. How are they similar? How are they different?

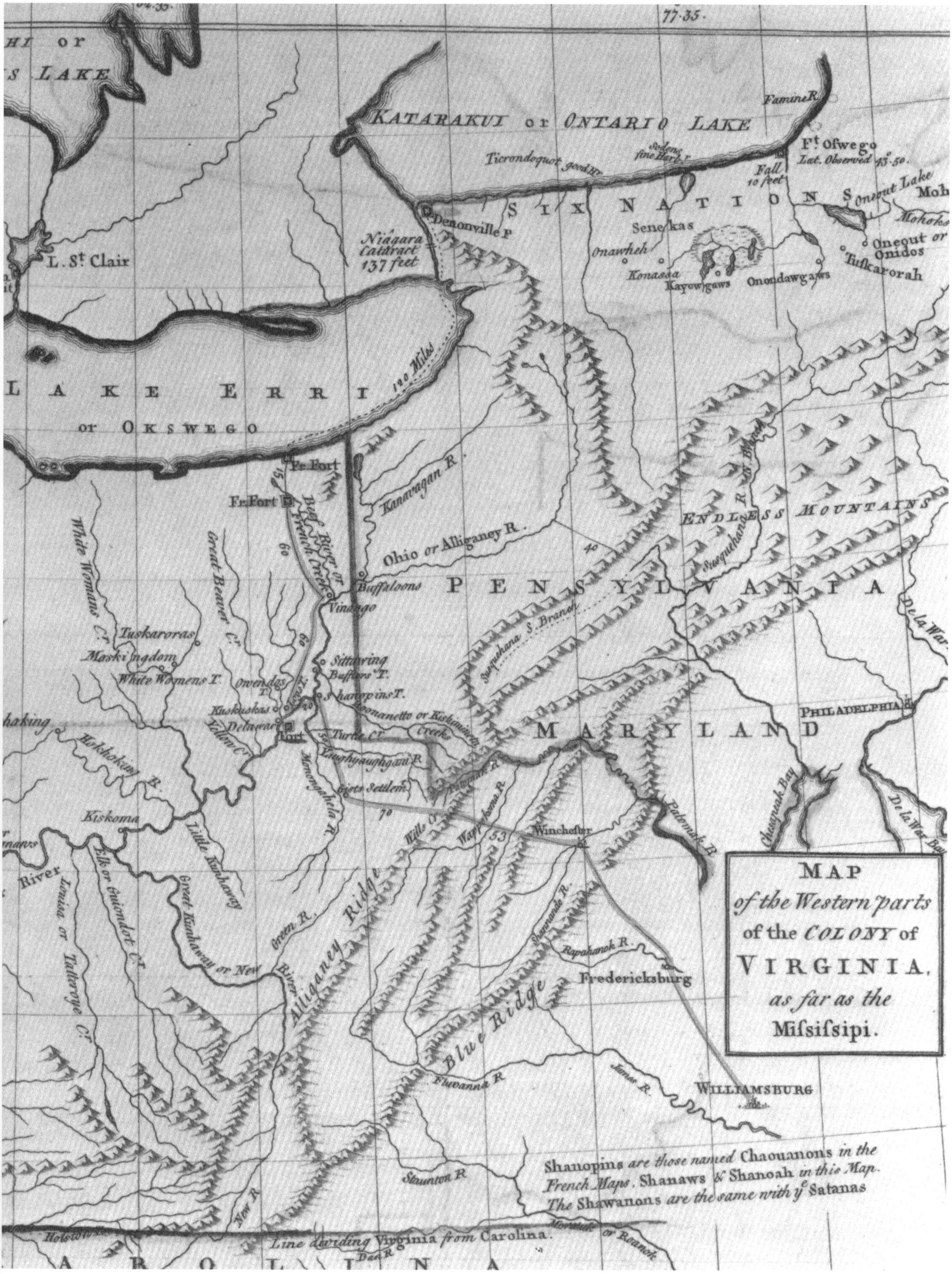
MAP
of the Western parts
of the COLONY of
VIRGINIA,
as far as the
Misisipi.
Shanopins are those named Chaouanons in the
French Maps, Shanaws & Shanoah in this Map.
The Shawanons are the same with ye Satanas
KATARAKUI or ONTARIO LAKE
LAKE ERRI
or OKSWEGO
SIX NATIONS
ENDLESS MOUNTAINS
PENSYLVANIA
MARYLAND
PHILADELPHIA
Ft. Oswego
Famine R.
Niagara Cattaract 137 feet
Denonville F.
L. St. Clair
Senekas
Onondawgaws
Tuskarorah
Fr. Fort
Buffaloons
Vinango
Ohio or Alliganey R.
Kanavagan R.
Winchester
Fredericksburg
WILLIAMSBURG
Blue Ridge
Alliganey Ridge
Rapahanok R.
Patomak R.
Chesapeak Bay
Fluvanna R.
James R.
Staunton R.
Great Kunhaway or New River
Line dividing Virginia from Carolina
77.35.

Mission to the Ohio,
Map Drawn by George Washington, 1753

While on a ***diplomatic*** mission to the Ohio frontier in 1753, George Washington used his skills as a ***surveyor*** to draw this map of the area. He mapped the region he traveled through and marked his route from Williamsburg, Virginia to the French forts in the Ohio River Valley (present day Pittsburgh, Pennsylvania area). His hand-drawn map was a detailed survey of the mountain ranges, rivers, and settlements of the western parts of the Virginia, Pennsylvania, and Maryland colonies. The map was published in George Washington's diary of his adventure, The Journal of Major Washington, in 1753. His map is so accurate in detail that it was later used when roads were planned in the 20th century.

Suggested Activities

Examine the map carefully. As a class, review the story of George Washington's mission to the Ohio Valley in 1753 on page 15.

1. Find the line that plots George Washington's route on his Mission to the Ohio. Record each stop he made on his journey. Can you find these settlements on a modern map?
2. How many mountain ranges and rivers did George Washington have to cross on his journey? Write a diary entry as George Washington describing a day of your journey to the Ohio Valley.
3. George Washington traveled with Native American guides through areas that were largely unsettled by whites in the 18th century. Examine the map carefully and record all settlements that have Native American names.
4. The area was largely controlled by the powerful Iroquois nation. Locate the names of the confederation tribes on the map and record them. Use your textbook or other sources to research information on each tribe George Washington listed on his map.
5. Use a modern map to plot George Washington's journey from Williamsburg to Pittsburgh. How many miles did he travel each way through the forests of the frontier?

thoſe countries, where all our ſciences had their birth.

VIRGINIA.

PETERSBURG, *Feb.* 15. On Saturday laſt a numerous and reſpectable company aſſembled at Mr. Robert Armiſtead's, to celebrate the birth of the illuſtrious GEORGE WASHINGTON, Eſquire. After dinner a ſong compoſed by a citizen of Peterſburg on the occaſion, was ſung, and (among others) the following toaſts were drank, attended with diſcharge of cannon, and a balloon was raiſed by a gentleman, which equally excited curioſity and applauſe.

His Excellency George Waſhington, Eſq. may his diſintereſted patriotiſm be handed down to the lateſt poſterity as a laſting monument of his memorable atchievements.

The United States of America, may they be as happy in peace as they have proved glorious in war.

His moſt Chriſtian Majeſty and the Queen of France, may deſpotiſm be taught a uſeful leſſon from their benevolent interpoſition to ſupport the rights of mankind.

The Marquis de la Fayette, whoſe illuſtrious exertions can only be exceeded by the goodneſs of his heart.

His Excellency JOHN HANCOCK, Eſq.

General Knox and the late American Army.

To the memory of the heroes who have fallen in the great cauſe of freedom.

PHILADELPHIA, March 1.

Extract of a letter from New-York

The Massachusetts Gazette, March 13, 1787

Today we celebrate Presidents' Day in February to honor George Washington and other presidents who have served our nation. The first public celebration of George Washington's birthday was held over 200 years ago by French officers to honor George Washington as the Commander in Chief of the American army during the Revolutionary War. Within a few years, Washington's birthday became an annual celebration in towns across the country. Balls, banquets, toasts, and speeches were given in his honor because Americans saw George Washington as the ***symbol*** of their union and independence.

Some people viewed George Washington's popularity with concern. They thought the public celebrations were like those offered for kings and it was hard for them to believe that, in a time when much of the world was ruled by kings, George Washington would not ***seize*** power. This newspaper account gives us a typical description of a dinner honoring George Washington on his birthday.

Although his birthday has been celebrated since the 1780s, it did not become an official holiday until 1885.

Suggested Activities

Read the newspaper article from the Massachusetts Gazette. Remember that in the colonial period the letter "s" was printed like the modern letter "f". Write down any word that you do not understand for class discussion.

1. In what city and state was the birthday celebration held for George Washington? Why do you think the news was published in a Massachusetts newspaper?

2. List three toasts that were offered at the birthday celebration for George Washington.

3. Write a poem or song the celebrates the accomplishments of George Washington in recognition of his birthday.

4. Divide into two groups. The first group should plan an 18th-century birthday party for George Washington. The second group should plan a modern birthday party for George Washington. Each group should include a menu of what will be served, decorations, entertainment, and special toasts in the style of your period. Share your celebration ideas with your classmates.

Negros

Belonging to George Washington in his own right and by Marriage

G.W

Names	ages	Remarks
Tradesmen &c.		
Nat - Smith		His wife Lucy - D.R. - do
George - Do		Ditto - Lydia R.T. - Do
Isaac - Carpr		... - Kitty Dairy - Do
James - Do	40	... - Darcus M.H. G.W
Sambo - Do		... - Agnes R.T. do
Davy - Do		... - Edy U.T. G.W
Joe - Do		... - Dolshy Spinr do
Tom - Coopr		... - Nanny M.H. G.W
Moses - Do		No Wife
Jacob - Do		Ditto
George - Gardr		His wife Sall - D.R. - do
Harry - Do		No wife
Boatswain Ditto		His wife Myrtilla Spinr G.W
Dundee - Do		His wife at Mr Lears
Charles - Do		Ditto - Fanny U.F. do
Ben - Do		Ditto - Peggy R.T. G.W
Ben - Miller		Ditto - Sinah Mn. H. do
Forester Do		No Wife
Nathan Cook	31	Wife - Peg - M.H. G.W
W. Muclus B. Layr		Do - Captn Marshall
Juba - Carter		No wife
Matilda Spinner		Boson - Ditcher
Frank H. Servt		Wife - Lucy - Cook
Will - Shoemr		Same - no wife
amount	24	

Dower

Names	ages	Remarks
Tradesmen &c.		
Tom Davis B. Layr		wife at Mr Lears
Simms - Carp		Do Daphne - French's
Cyrus - Postn		Do Lucy R.T. - G.W
Wilson - Ditto	15	No wife
Godfrey Cartr		Wife - Mima Mn H. do
James - Do		Do - Alla - Do - do
Hanson - Distr		No wife
Peter - Do		Ditto
Nat - Do		Ditto
Daniel - Do		Ditto
Timothy - Do		
Ha: Joe - Ditchr		Wife Sylla D.R. - G.W
Christr - H. Servt		Do May Wests
Marcus - Do		No Wife
Lucy - Cook		Husbd H. Frank - G.W
Charlotte - Sempst		No Husband
Sall - H. Md		Do
Caroline - Do		Husbd Peter Hardman
Kitty - Milkmd		Do Isaac Carpr G.W
Alce - Spinr		Charles Freeman
Betty Davis - Do		Mrs Washington's Dick
Dolshy		Husbd Joe Carpr G.W
Anna		Do lives at George Town
Judy	21	No Husband
Delphy		Ditto - do
Peter Lam Knittr		No wife
Alla - Do		Husbd James Cartr dower
amount	28	

Mansion House — Passed Labour (G.W)

Names	ages	Remarks
Frank	80	No Wife
Gunner	90	Wife - Judy - R.T. G.W
Sam - Cook	40	Ditto Alce M.H. Do

Mansion House (Dower)

Names	ages	Remarks
Will		Wife Aggy D.R. G.W
Joe - Postiln		Do - Sall R.T. - Do
Mike		No wife - son to Lucy
Sinah		Husbd Miller Ben - G.W
Mima		Do - Godfrey Wagr - do
Lucy		No Husband
Grace		Husbd Mr Lear's - Juba

Census of Slaves at Mount Vernon, 1799

Before George Washington prepared his will, he made a list of slaves living at Mount Vernon. The slaves were divided into two categories: slaves belonging to General Washington and "dower" slaves who belonged to the estate of Martha Washington's first husband, Daniel Parke Custis. By law, the "dower" slaves did not legally belong to George Washington but to the ***heirs*** of Daniel Custis. George Washington could not free the "dower" slaves because they did not belong to him.

The census is a very important document. It tells the names and jobs of every slave that lived and worked at Mount Vernon. It also tells historians about families on the estate. By reading the census you can learn, for example, that about 2/3 of the adult slaves at Mount Vernon were married and of those 96 people, only 36 lived in the same household as their husband or wife and their children. Many slaves lived and worked at different farms at Mount Vernon than their spouse. Some were married to slaves that lived on other plantations near Mount Vernon.

Suggested Activities

Read over the census carefully.

1. With your group, create a chart listing the following information:

   How many male slaves are listed
   How many female slaves are listed
   How many children are listed
   How many slaves belonged to George Washington
   How many slaves are listed as "dower" slaves
   How many different trades or skilled laborers are listed
   How many different farms where people lived are listed

2. The laws of Virginia in the late 18th century did not recognize marriage between slaves. Can you find any evidence that George Washington did recognize slave marriages? What is that evidence?

3. Choose one skill or trade listed on the slave census. Research that trade and explain to your classmates the job that person did at Mount Vernon.

4. Are there any married slaves listed on the census where one spouse belonged to George Washington and one spouse was a "dower" slave? Discuss what happened when George Washington freed his slaves and the "dower" slaves remained enslaved at Mount Vernon. Write a letter or essay from the point of view of one of these family members. Are you happy that freedom has been granted? How do you feel that your husband, wife, or children must remain slaves, however?

Activities and Puzzles

George Washington's Life: A Crossword Puzzle

ACROSS
1. George Washington's eldest half brother.
3. Favorite smoked meat.
6. River at Mount Vernon.
10. George Washington's step-daughter.
11. Frozen water.
13. First U.S. President.
16. Wood sources.
17. Food from river.
20. Common food preservative.
21. George Washington's rank.
22. Cob of corn.
25. George Washington's step-grandson.
26. Pennsylvania winter encampment.
27. George Washington's stepson.
28. Early U.S. Capital City.
29. Head coverings.
30. General Washington's close friend from France.

DOWN
2. Mrs. Washington's first husband.
4. George Washington's Virginia home.
5. Water transportation.
7. Farm managers.
8. Farm animals, part horse.
9. Mrs. Washington's first name.
10. Large farm.
12. Latest information.
14. Pretty, fragrant flower.
15. Short message.
18. Theater performance.
19. George Washington's step-granddaughter.
23. George Washington's main cash crop.
24. Favorite afternoon beverage.
25. Spun from sheep's coat.

Hoe Cake Recipe

George Washington's favorite breakfast was cornmeal pancakes, then called "hoe cakes" because they were cooked over an open fire on a long-handled metal tool that looked like a hoe. Washington poured honey over his hoe cakes and completed his breakfast with hot tea. The precise recipe that was used in Washington's kitchen is not known, but one adapted from the period follows:

2 cups milk	1 cup cornmeal	2 beaten eggs
1/2 teaspoon salt	4 tablespoons honey	1 cup flour

Mix together the cornmeal, flour and salt. Heat the milk until it just begins to boil (steam appears) and pour it in the dry mixture. Add the honey and eggs. Stir just until the ingredients are wet. Spoon the batter onto a hot, oiled griddle and cook like pancakes, turning to brown both sides.

Washington Word Search

L	G	E	C	I	V	I	L	I	T	Y	W	I	M	K
W	A	E	V	P	H	V	G	O	O	H	N	A	Y	M
A	K	R	O	A	V	J	H	W	E	D	N	S	Y	N
S	O	I	E	R	L	P	D	A	I	S	N	I	C	O
H	O	F	N	N	G	S	T	A	I	O	K	O	A	I
I	B	W	I	A	E	E	N	O	I	S	U	U	R	T
N	Y	M	M	P	U	G	N	T	K	L	N	Q	C	U
G	P	U	L	F	E	G	U	L	R	A	A	O	O	L
T	O	L	A	N	E	T	U	B	A	X	I	R	M	O
O	C	R	V	U	I	N	J	R	A	H	Y	I	E	V
N	M	O	L	T	Y	Q	E	E	A	T	T	M	D	E
C	Y	O	S	P	B	K	T	H	V	T	T	R	R	R
P	G	N	C	O	N	G	R	E	S	S	I	L	A	A
Y	O	L	Y	N	E	H	G	E	L	L	A	O	E	M
C	H	P	N	O	I	T	A	T	N	A	L	P	N	J

Allegheny
army
battle
civility
Congress
Constitution
copybook
democracy
envoy
eulogy
farm
General
George
inauguration
Indian
Iroquois
mansion
Martha
plantation
Revolution
slave
Washington
wheat

Mount Vernon Word Search

G E O R G E W A S H I N G T O N
K L C A S H C R O P X M Q S E I N E S A P P
B M A R T H A C U S T I S W L M U L E S N I
P C A N D L E S B I T I C E O L J A C K Y X A S
N C H O E C A K E S A P A T S Y W H E A T Z Z U
H O G E N E R A L B O W L I N G G R E E N Z R
A C U P O L A M X P L A N T A T I O N Y Q A A V
M A N S I O N L O V E R S E E R P O T O M A C E
F A R M E R X W A S H Y M O U N T V E R N O N Y

bowling green
candles
canoe
cash crop
cupola
farmer
garden

General
George Washington
ham
hoe cakes
ice
Jacky
mansion

Martha Custis
Mount Vernon
mules
Nelly
overseer
Patsy
piazza

plantation
Potomac
seines
stable
survey
Washy
wheat

A Brief Biography of George Washington

Part I: A Colonial Boyhood

People from many countries settled in early America. Among them was John Washington. He sailed to Virginia from England in 1657 on a ship called the Sea Horse of London. In a few years, John Washington acquired land, married, and began a family. His most famous ***descendant*** was his great-grandson, George Washington, the first President of the United States.

George Washington was born at ten o'clock in the morning on February 22, 1732, in Westmoreland County, Virginia. His parents were Augustine and Mary Ball Washington. George grew up near Fredericksburg, Virginia. He had a younger sister and three younger brothers. He also had two older half brothers who were sent to England to go to school.

Studying was very important. Spelling and handwriting were practiced be writing in a ***copybook***. Children copied the "Rules of Civility," which told them how to behave. George carefully wrote all 110 rules in his copybook which helped him to develop good handwriting. He worked hard and learned about geography, astronomy, arithmetic and ***surveying***.

When George was 11 years old, his father died. George became very close to his older half brother, Lawrence. George liked to visit Lawrence who was living in a small house built on the Potomac River. Lawrence named the house and its farm, Mount Vernon.

George enjoyed listening to Lawrence talk about time he served in the military with the British. He also liked to hear Lawrence and his friends talk about the Virginia ***frontier***. One day, George learned that Lawrence's friend, George William Fairfax, was going to the frontier to survey land. George wanted to go. He had learned a little about surveying and had practiced by measuring Lawrence's turnip field. Although he was only 16 years old, Mr. Fairfax allowed him to join the group.

George learned more than surveying on the trip. The men rode on horseback for days exploring the wilderness. They slept in the open, still wearing their clothes and rolled up in blankets. They talked with Indians, ate some of their food, and watched them dance in the bright firelight. George wrote about these ***experiences*** in his journal.

Discussion Topics

1. Do you study the same things that Washington did as a boy? What do you study that Washington did not? Why do you think what children study has changed? Do teachers and parents still have rules for good behavior?

2. What do you think Washington's surveying trip was like? Would it be similar to a trip to the Shenandoah Valley today? How would it be different? How do you think Washington crossed rivers? Would there have been roads and hotels?

Also See

Page 14, "Rules of Civility," which provides a facsimile of Washington's boyhood handwriting from the Rules of Civility, with suggested activities

George became a good surveyor. He started his own business when he was 17 years old. He was honest and fair, many people hired him to survey their lands.

When George was 19, his older half brother, Lawrence, became very ill. Many doctors tried to cure him, but nothing helped. After Lawrence's death, George lived at Mount Vernon.

George joined the Virginia ***militia***. He was sent to the Ohio River on an important mission by the British governor of Virginia. Soon Major Washington was fighting in the first battles of the French and Indian War. The next year, he served as an ***aide*** to the British General Edward Braddock. In a fearful battle, George Washington escaped injury many times. Four bullets ripped through his coat. Two horses were shot from under him. Later, he was made a colonel and led soldiers who ***defended*** Virginia's frontier in the Shenandoah Valley. Finally, after years of battles and a British victory, the war was over.

About this time, Colonel Washington met a young woman named Martha Custis. Her husband had died, leaving her with two small children, Jacky, three years old, and Patsy, one year old. George Washington and Martha Custis were married on January 6, 1759.

The Washingtons were happy at Mount Vernon. Many friends and relatives visited,. There were parties and foxhunts. Colonel Washington had already added on to the house and now bought land to increase the size of his plantation. He grew many food crops. He stopped growing tobacco and made wheat and corn his main ***cash crops***.

Colonel Washington was elected to the House of Burgesses and often went to its meetings in the Virginia capital of Williamsburg. He was quiet and thoughtful during the meetings. One person described him as "straight as an Indian,...more than six feet two inches...about 175 pounds." His hair was reddish brown and his eyes were blue. While in Williamsburg, he and Martha would go to concerts and plays. They liked to dance and went to fancy balls at the Governor's Palace.

Discussion Topics

1. Why do you think being honest and fair helped Washington as a surveyor? Would people buy land if they thought it was surveyed incorrectly? Is being honest and fair important for surveyors today? Is it important in other jobs? Why?

2. Why do you think Washington grew many food crops at Mount Vernon? Could he buy food at a grocery store? How was food cooked then? How do you think people kept food from spoiling?

Also see:

Page 15, "1753: George Washington's Mission to the Ohio," for an account of this trip.

Page 19, "George Washington and Slavery," for a discussion of Washington's changing attitude toward slavery that ultimately led him to free his slaves.

Please Help Us Evaluate the George Washington Lesson Date: ____

Name: ____ Phone: ____

School Name: ____ Grade: ____

School Address: ____ City: ____ State: ____ Zip: ____

	Not Used	Used		Not Used	Used
Biography for Teachers	❑	❑	Rebellion in the Army	❑	❑
Student Biography *	❑	❑	Reluctant President	❑	❑
GW and Slavery	❑	❑	Mission to the Ohio	❑	❑
GW and Art	❑	❑	Journal Activities	❑	❑
Primary Document Lesson	❑	❑	Scratch and Learn Cards	❑	❑
Rules of Civility	❑	❑	Trading Cards	❑	❑

*Students Read ❑

Activities: Crossword ❑ Word Search ❑ Other ❑

These materials were ❑ not at all useful ❑ somewhat useful ❑ very useful

These materials ❑ do not correspond ❑ do correspond with the Standards of Learning in my State.

...Goods from ...heir crops to ...igher taxes.

...to discuss the ...75, Colonel ...battles had been ...ad started. A ...*der in Chief* of the

...have enough ...to make the most of ...Vashington ...the British directly. ...sh could not capture ...e British General

Although the war was won, it was also a sad time for the Washington family. Martha's son, Jacky, died of Camp Fever at Yorktown. Her daughter, Patsy, had died a few years earlier.

In 1783 a peace treaty with England was signed. Some of General Washington's officers wanted him to ***seize*** power and run the new nation, but he refused. Instead he resigned as Commander in Chief, disbanded the Army, and went home to Mount Vernon to live the rest of his life as a private citizen.

However, this was not to be. The 13 new states did not work well together. Soon each state sent delegates to a Constitutional Convention in Philadelphia to solve the problem. General Washington went and asked to ***preside*** over the convention. After weeks of long ***debates*** and many votes, the ***delegates*** worked out their differences. They wrote a new constitution for the nation with a ***democratic*** government. When the time came to elect a new a leader for the new government, George Washington was the ***unanimous*** choice.

Discussion Topics

1. Why do you think Washington's men wanted to seize power? Would they become rich and powerful? What would have happened to other people and to the country? Why do you think Washington stopped his men? What do you think he wanted for the country?
2. Why do you think the states did not work well together? At that time they all had different money and different laws. How would you buy something in another place if your money was not good there? What would be a better solution?

Also See

Page 16, "Rebellion in the Continental Army!" for a mock-up newspaper account of Washington's confrontation with the officers who wanted to seize power.

Part IV: President and Back Home

In New York City on April 30, 1789, George Washington took the oath of office as President of the United States. An excited crowd gave three rousing cheers. Those early years were very important to our new country. President Washington felt he had to be very careful so the new government would succeed. He worked very hard. He created ***departments*** within the government, each with a different job. He made sure that federal laws were obeyed everywhere. He had the government issue money that was good in all the states. President Washington also helped plan a new capital for the nation that was named "Washington" in his honor. Many of his decisions became ***precedents*** that later presidents would follow.

Washington agreed to serve a second term as president, even though he wanted to go home to Mount Vernon. Some people wanted him to be president even longer, but he would not. After eight years he left the office to the newly elected president, John Adams.

Once again called General Washington, as he liked, he returned home. At last he was able to take care of his ***beloved*** Mount Vernon plantation. Once more family and friends visited for dinner, conversation, and dancing.

General Washington enjoyed quiet evenings on the piazza overlooking the Potomac River. One of Martha's grandchildren , Nelly, often played music for him and his guests. This peaceful life lasted less than three years.

After riding through a bad winter storm, General Washington caught a cold. His throat became ***infected*** making it difficult to breathe. On December 14, 1799, at the age of 67, George Washington died from this infection called ***quinsy***. As he wished, he was buried at Mount Vernon.

People everywhere ***mourned***. Henry Lee, who had bee with Washington in the Revolutionary War, wrote that Washington was"...first in war, first in peace and first in the hearts of his countrymen." General Lee read this ***eulogy*** in Congress. Everyone shared his feelings.

Discussion Topics

1. Why do you think the first years of the new government, when Washington was President, were so important? What would have happened to the country if the government Washington set up had failed? Would that have made a difference to us today? Do you think he was a successful president?

2 Why were people sad when Washington died? How can someone be "first in war" and "first in peace" at the same time? What do these words mean? If you were to write a Eulogy for yourself, what would it be?

Also See

"The Reluctant President," page 17, for a discussion of Washington's feelings about being elected president.

GEORGE WASHINGTON: PIONEER FARMER

Scratch and Learn Card Answer Key

If you asked George Washington his occupation, he would have replied, "farmer." Even when away at war and during the presidency, Washington oversaw and kept meticulous records of work on Mount Vernon's five farms. He was an innovative leader among the progressive farmers of his time, whose ideas introduced scientific methods to farming and revolutionized American agriculture.

A.

B.

	Year #1	Year #2	Year #3	Year #4	Year #5	Year #6	Year #7
Field #1	Corn & Potatoes	Pasture/ Grasses	Pasture/ Grasses	Oats & Buckwheat	Wheat	Buckwheat	Wheat
Field #2	Wheat	Corn & Potatoes	Pasture/ Grasses	Pasture/ Grasses	Oats & Buckwheat	Wheat	Buckwheat
Field #3	Buckwheat	Wheat	Corn & Potatoes	Pasture/ Grasses	Pasture/ Grasses	Oats & Buckwheat	Wheat
Field #4	Wheat	Buckwheat	Wheat	Corn & Potatoes	Pasture/ Grasses	Pasture/ Grasses	Oats & Buckwheat
Field #5	Oats & Buckwheat	Wheat	Buckwheat	Wheat	Corn & Potatoes	Pasture/ Grasses	Pasture/ Grasses
Field #6	Pasture/ Grasses	Oats & Buckwheat	Wheat	Buckwheat	Wheat	Corn & Potatoes	Pasture/ Grasses
Field #7	Pasture/ Grasses	Pasture/ Grasses	Oats & Buckwheat	Wheat	Buckwheat	Wheat	Corn & Potatoes

C.

D.

E.

A. **Spikey Roller**: Washington continually experimented with the latest technology in farming. The Spikey Roller - a log roller with iron spikes - was used to loosen the ground for deep plowing. Washington also invented a "barrel seeder" which planted seeds in regular rows.

B. **Wheat**: Washington recognized the drawbacks of tobacco, the traditional cash crop of Virginia. It quickly depleted the soil's nutrients, increased soil erosion, and required a large workforce. Washington switched to wheat, which he could sell locally as well as overseas. He then built a grist mill and was able to sell wheat as flour as well as grain.

C. **Crop Rotation**: Most Virginia planters cleared new land as fields became exhausted from tobacco and overuse. Washington believed this was wasteful and instituted a seven year crop rotation system which restored the productivity of Mount Vernon's fields.

D. **Sixteen-Sided Treading Barn**: Washington designed and built an innovative 16-sided barn for threshing wheat. In his design, livestock walked on the wheat on the upper level - as the grain was treaded out, it fell through the gaps between the floorboards to the lower level where it was gathered and stored.

E. **Mule**: George Washington was instrumental in introducing the mule, the offspring of a horse and a donkey, to America. He found that mules were hardworking and less expensive to maintain than horses. Mules soon became a common work animal in America.

SCRATCH AND LEARN CARDS

The ten statements on each scratch and learn card are printed below. The answer choices are printed to the right, with the correct ones in boldface type. The correct answers can be found by reading "A Brief Biography of George Washington" on pages 3 through 6. Have your students complete the scratch and learn cards in a way you think will be most effective: individually, in groups, with the Biography or without.

1. George Washington was born in:	**Virginia**	New York	Massachusetts
2. *Rules of Civility* taught Washington how to:	Brag	Subtract	**Behave**
3. As a surveyor, Washington was:	Fast	**Honest**	Sloppy
4. Washington married:	Mary Ball Washington	Nelly Custis	**Martha Custis**
5. One of Washington's main cash crops was:	Peas	**Wheat**	Cotton
6. Washington and other colonists became unhappy with England because of:	**Taxes**	Schools	Food
7. After the Revolution was won, Washington:	Seized Power	Was Fired	**Resigned**
8. Washington and the state delegates agreed on the U. S. Constitution by:	Fighting	Giving In	**Voting**
9. Washington was President of the U.S. for	**8 Years**	Life	4 Years
10. George Washington was buried at:	Washington D.C.	**Mount Vernon**	Fredericksburg

Activity Solutions

Washington Word Search

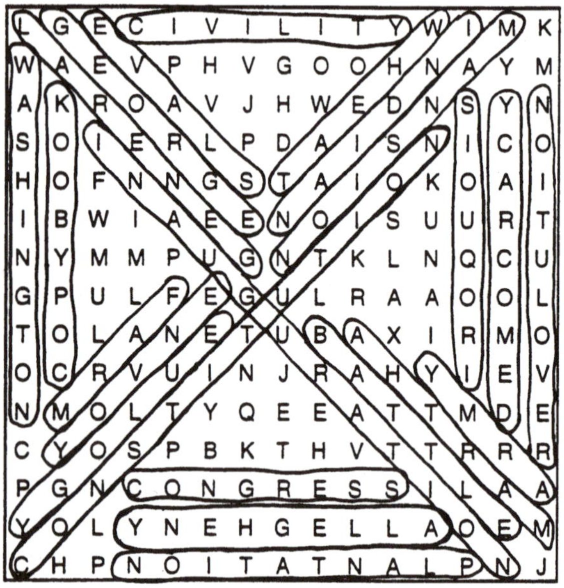

Mount Vernon Word Search

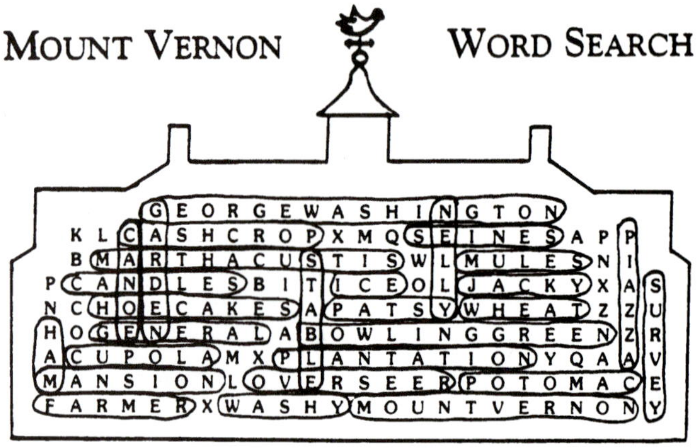

George Washington's Life: A Crossword Puzzle

Students' Reading List

Brandt, Keith. *George Washington.* Mahwah, New Jersey: Troll Associates, 1985.
Cunliffe, Marcus. *George Washington and the Making of a Nation.* American Heritage Junior Library. New York: American Heritage Publishing Company, 1966.
Collier, James Lincoln and Collier, Christopher. *My Brother Sam is Dead.* New York: Scholastic, Inc. 1974.
Davis, Burke. *Black Heroes of the American Revolution.* New York: Harcourt Brace Jovanovich, 1976.
Fleming, James Thomas. *First in Their Hearts: A Biography of George Washington.* New York: Walkerand Co., 1984.
Fritz, Jean. *George Washington's Breakfast.* New York: McCann, Inc., 1969.
McGovern, Ann. *The Secret Soldier: The Story of Deborah Sampson.* New York: Scholastic, Inc., 1975.
Meltzer, M. *George Washington and the Birth of Our Nation.* New York: Dell Publishing, 1988.
Milton, J. *The Story of George Washington, Quiet Hero.* New York: Dell Publishing, 1988.
Mount Vernon Ladies' Association. *George Washington Pioneer Farmer Coloring and Game Book.* Mount Vernon, Virginia: The Founders, 1996.
Reit, Seymour. *Guns for General Washington: A Story of the American Revolution.* New York: Harcourt Brace Jovanovich, 1990.
Wagoner, J.B. *Martha Washington: America's First Lady.* New York: Aladdin Paperbacks, 1986.
Washington, George. *The Journal of Major Washington, Sent by the Hon. Robert Dinwiddie...to the French Forces on the Ohio.* Facsimile Edition. Williamsburg, Virginia: Colonial Williamsburg Foundation, 1991.
Washington, George. *Rules of Civility and Decent Behavior in Company and Conversation.* Mount Vernon, Virginia: Mount Vernon Ladies' Association, 1989.

Teachers' Reading List

Abbot, W.W., and D. Twohig, ed. *The Papers of George Washington.* Chalottesville, Virginia: University Press of Virginia, 1983.
Alden, J.R. *George Washington, A Biography.* Baton Rouge, Louisiana: Louisiana State University Press, 1984.
Brookhiser, Richard. *Founding Father: Rediscovering George Washington.* New York: The Free Press, 1996.
Cunliffe, Marcus. *George Washington: Man and Monument.* Mount Vernon, Virginia: The Mount Vernon Ladies' Association, 1998.
Fields, J.E. *Worthy Partner: The Papers of Martha Washington.* Westport, Connecticut: Greenwood Press, 1994.
Flexner, Thomas J. *Washington: The Indispensable Man.* Boston: Little, Brown, 1976.
Higgonbotham, Donald. *George Washington and the American Military Tradition.* Athens, Georgia: University Press of Georgia Press, 1985.
Jackson, D., and Twohig, Dorothy, ed. *The Diaries of George Washington.* Charlottesville, Virginia: University Press of Virginia, 1976-1979.
Morgan, Edmund. *The Genius of George Washington.* New York: Norton, 1981.
Mount Vernon Ladies' Association. *Mount Vernon: A Handbook.* Mount Vernon, Virginia: The Mount Vernon Ladies' Association, 1985.
Palmer, Dave R. *George Washington: First in War.* Mount Vernon, Virginia: The Mount Vernon Ladies' Association, 2000.
Quarles, Benjamin. *The Negro in the American Revolution.* New York: W.W. Norton & Co., 1973.
Washington, George. *The Last Will and Testament of George Washington.* Mount Vernon, Virginia: The Mount Vernon Ladies' Association, 1939.

Other Resources

Dig Into George Washington CD-ROM offers video tours of 12 rooms of Washington's home, audio quotes from Washington's papers, a virtual tour of the outbuildings at Mount Vernon, an interactive section on slave life at Mount Vernon, and an in-depth look at the use of archaeology to interpret history. Also includes 12 lesson plans on PDF files. The Mount Vernon Ladies' Association, 1998.

The Life of George Washington. 30-minute VHS videotape. The Mount Vernon Ladies' Association, 1990.

Mount Vernon: The Home of George Washington. 30-minute VHS videotape. The Mount Vernon Ladies' Association, 1990.

Songs from the American Revolution. Song book by Kate Van Winkle Keller. Connecticut: The Hendrickson Group, 1992.

Internet Sites

Mount Vernon Estate and Gardens:
http://www.mountvernon.org

The Papers of George Washington:
www.virginia.edu/gwpapers

Library of Congress – Washington Papers
http://lcweb2.loc.gov/ammem/gwhtml/gwhome.html

The Access Indiana Teaching and Learning Center
http://tlc.ai.org/washindx.htm

Valley Forge Historical Society
http://www.ushistory.org/valleyforge